FATAL SUNSET:
DEADLY VACATIONS

MARK YOSHIMOTO NEMCOFF

Glenneyre Press
Los Angeles, CA

Copyright © 2012 Mark Yoshimoto Nemcoff. All rights reserved, including the right to reproduce this book, or portions thereof, in any form. No part of this text may be reproduced, transmitted, downloaded, decompiled, reverse engineered, or stored in or introduced into any information storage and retrieval system, in any form or by any means, whether electronic or mechanical without the express written permission of the author. The scanning, uploading, and distribution of this book via the internet or via any other means without the permission of the publisher is illegal and punishable by law.

ISBN: 1-934602-16-7
ISBN-13: 978-1-934602-16-4

Published by Glenneyre Press, LLC.
Los Angeles, CA
www.wordsushi.com

First Edition

Cover design and photo by: MYN

FATAL SUNSET is dedicated to the memories of Nolan Webster, David Potts, Brent Midlocks and the many victims whose tragic stories are chronicled in this book.

I am not telling you to avoid going on vacation. Nor am I trying to suggest you shouldn't go to Mexico, the Caribbean, Hawaii or on a cruise.

This book only asks one thing:

DARE TO BE AWARE!

TABLE OF CONTENTS:

INTRODUCTION
1

CRUISE SHIP DISAPPEARANCES
4

WHAT HAPPENED ABOARD THE COSTA CONCORDIA?
21

MEXICODE RED
32

INTERVIEW WITH MAUREEN WEBSTER
53

FLORIDA: THE GUNSHINE STATE
58

CARIBBEAN DREAMS GONE BAD
73

THE NATALEE HOLLOWAY DISAPPEARANCE: EVERY PARENT'S NIGHTMARE
83

ALOHA MEANS GOODBYE
102

TOP 10 "DARE TO BE AWARE" TRAVEL TIPS I LEARNED WRITING FATAL SUNSET
123

INTRODUCTION

Vacation is the ointment of the soul.

There are few things we love more than leaving behind the grind of our daily lives and heading off for a few days to get away from it all—to relax, have fun, maybe take in the sights. Rarely, when we are thinking about those warm sandy beaches, snorkeling trips and drinks on the lanai, do we ever contemplate the notion that paradise could potentially be the location of sudden and unexpected tragedy.

I was two days into a Maui vacation with my family when I first heard news of David Potts. Barely a dozen miles from where I was staying, Potts had been knocked down by a large wave, which then very quickly washed him twenty feet into the narrow, lava-rock rimmed Nakalele Point Blowhole. Instantly, his body was pulled deep into the churning current below the jagged lava rock shelf and never seen again.

As unsuccessful searches for David Potts, and later his body, continued to make the local paper, I thought to myself that in the times I'd been to Maui, not once had I ever heard a single person make mention of the potential, yet somewhat seemingly obvious, danger of getting too close to this particular natural attraction. I'm the kind of person who, for a photo or a dare, would probably have done the same thing as David Potts. I don't blame his death on stupidity or carelessness. I think that we often go on vacation and conveniently forget that we may be taking risks that are beyond our capacity to handle when the situation very quickly goes from serene to adverse.

My intent in writing FATAL SUNSET is not to sensationalize the tragic deaths of unfortunate vacation-goers, but instead to point out that your carefree getaway is not immune to danger whether it is from forces of nature beyond your control or predators who count on the fact that your guard may be down.

Though I have found nearly all of the stories mentioned in this book to be somewhat terrifying in their own rights, it does not mean I will forgo my family vacations in order to hide in the relative safety of my own house. Instead, in the same way that I always look both ways before crossing the street, I feel that when armed with knowledge of events past I am better prepared to identify potential hazardous situations and hopefully avoid similar tragedies befalling myself and those I care dearly about.

Should you be afraid to go to any of the places mentioned in this book? No. But you have to remember it's not always rainbows and Mai Tais. You should be aware of the potential dangers. In the name of having fun, you may undertake some physical challenges that you are unprepared for or may visit places you believe are safer than they seem. For me, personally, knowing what I know now will make my vacations even better. At the very least, I'd like to think my vacations will be safer for my entire family…and will help us continue to enjoy happy memories intended to last a lifetime.

CRUISE SHIP DISAPPEARANCES

Though it is quite uncommon to hear about the type of fatal incident that doomed the Costa *Concordia* (on a Friday the 13th, no less), it is surprisingly even more rare to hear anyone talk about the alarming statistics involving people who have gone missing from perfectly sound and functional cruise ships.

According to the U.S.-based International Cruise Victim's Association—set up by businessman Kendall Carver after his own daughter, Merrian, disappeared from a cruise—more than one hundred seventy people have gone missing at sea since 1995.

Twenty-four passengers disappeared between 2003 and 2006, not including suicides and accidents due to intoxication. More than thirty passengers mysteriously vanished from cruise ships without a trace since 2007. Thirteen of those in 2011, alone.

It is an increasing trend with disturbing and somewhat sinister implications.

It was August of 2004 that Kendall Carver received a frantic call from his thirteen-year-old granddaughter asking, "Do you know where my mommy is? I've been trying to call her and she hasn't called back for days. Is she with you?"

What Carver didn't know was that Merrian, a vivacious forty-year-old redhead with a penchant for writing poetry, had taken a flight from Boston to Seattle before boarding the cruise ship *Mercury* on a seven-day Alaskan Royal Caribbean vacation without telling anyone, not even her own daughter.

And then without a trace, Merrian Carver vanished at sea.

By the second day of the cruise, a ship attendant named Domingo Monterio noticed the bed in Merrian's cabin had gone unused. After reporting this to his supervisor, Monterio was instructed to, "Just forget about it and do your job."

For six more nights, the attendant continued to place the customary chocolates on Merrian's pillow in the bed that remained empty for the remainder of the cruise.

Three weeks after the *Mercury* docked in Vancouver, Kendall Carver called the cruise line. After three additional days, Royal Caribbean officials finally confirmed that Merrian had boarded the vessel. However, what they couldn't tell him was where she had gotten off, or if she had even gotten off at all.

In fact, it seemed to Kendall Carver that Royal Caribbean had known all along that Merrian had not once disembarked from the *Mercury* after discovering what her cabin attendant had reported to his own boss. Even when everyone else had left the ship in Vancouver harbor, all of Merrian's belongings remained in her cabin.

Then to Kendall Carver's horror, he was informed that all of Merrian's clothing had been given to charity and that her purse containing all of her identification and Social Security card was locked up in storage. Most shocking of all, Royal Caribbean never informed anyone, neither the police nor her family, of Merrian's strange disappearing act.

Two months after Merrian vanished, Carver hired Tim Schmolder, a San Francisco-based private investigator to discover exactly what happened to his daughter. However, once Schmolder began asking questions, Royal Caribbean put up roadblocks stymieing the investigation. Schmolder's requests to interview passengers and crew were denied. His access to investigate the ship's video surveillance tapes was blocked. Initially, cruise officials told Carver that video tapes were erased after twelve days when in fact it was company policy to keep them for thirty days. By the time Carver learned the truth, it was too late. The tapes had been wiped clean.

After much pressure, Schmolder was eventually allowed two hours to "walk through" the *Mercury*. He checked out Merrian's room on the Panorama Deck, more than one hundred feet above the waterline. Although her cabin had an ocean view, the windows were bolted shut. Still, Schmolder easily saw that her room was a short distance to an elevator or stairs leading up to an open-air deck.

"It seemed highly plausible that someone could go overboard without being observed," Schmolder reported, adding that Merrian's "sudden disappearance is most easily explained by the suicide theory."

However, Schmolder could not positively rule out foul play aboard the *Mercury*. "A harmful encounter with a stranger would almost certainly have been swift and fatal."

Desperate for any clues, the Carvers' attorneys forced Royal Caribbean to make cabin attendant Domingo Montiero available for questioning. What was said in Montiero's deposition now opened the doors for the discovery of Royal Caribbean's own documents offering possible evidence that Merrian's disappearance had been covered up. Montiero's report of the suspicious circumstances of Merrian's room had been logged, along with documentation showing Royal Caribbean had held their own internal investigation, which eventually led to the firing of Montiero's boss over his handling of the situation.

In the three months since Kendal Carver began asking questions, not once did Royal Caribbean officials divulge any of that information. Ship records confirmed that Merrian had never utilized her Sea Pass, an onboard credit card that also acts as passenger identification. Never had it been used by Merrian to buy a single drink or make any other purchase. There also was no record that Merrian left the ship in any port during the cruise.

Almost exactly one year later, in August of 2005, the Carvers sued Royal Caribbean for damages.

When reporters began to question the cruise line's officials about both the lawsuit and Merrian's disappearance, Royal Caribbean issued a short statement on October 26:

"Mrs. Carver had severe emotional problems, had attempted suicide before and appears to have committed suicide on our ship. The death of Merrian Carver is a horrible tragedy, but, regrettably, there is very little a cruise line, a resort or a hotel can do to prevent someone from committing suicide."

Stunned and insulted by the press release, Kendall Carver asked, "How do they know she's dead? Do they know something we don't?"

The strange and mysterious case of Merrian Carver is not the only time Royal Caribbean has been accused of a cover-up in an attempt to protect the cruise line's image and legal interests. On March 24, 1998, twenty-three year old Amy Lynn Bradley also disappeared without a trace while traveling aboard the Royal Caribbean ship, *Rhapsody of the Seas* with her mother, father and brother.

Amy was a pretty, recent college graduate who attracted the attention of several crewmembers aboard the ship. According to her mother, "The waiters were very over-attentive towards Amy from the moment they met her. After dinner one evening, one of the waiters approached us while we were visiting with associates with whom we had been traveling and asked for Amy by name. The waiter stated 'they' wanted to take Amy to Carlos and Charlie's while docked in Aruba."

This was an invitation Amy chose to not only pass on, but also to not even acknowledge. "I would never do anything with any of those crewmembers. They give me the creeps," Amy responded. Instead, she and her brother chose to stay aboard the *Rhapsody of the Seas* instead of exploring Aruba.

"That same evening, March 23 (Monday), while docked in Aruba," added Amy's Mother, "all four of us attended a party on the upper deck, where the band was playing. We noticed a group of individuals standing alongside the railing who had boarded the ship with a dance troupe and who also were not passengers. They were not a part of the cruise! I wondered, how they could be allowed to board a ship and just stand around watching the performance with paying passengers? Looking back now, it seems even more dangerous to us."

Shortly afterwards, the Bradleys noticed something quite curious, and now-seemingly ominous. During the party, Amy and her mother ventured to the ship's fourth deck to check out photos that had been taken after dinner by the ship's photographer. To their surprise, every single one of Amy's photos was missing. Though the photographer claimed he remembered placing them out in the gallery where all of the other passenger photos were on display, the pictures had vanished.

The following day, during the early morning hours, Amy Lynn Bradley left her cabin with only her cigarettes and a lighter and was never seen again.

According to her mother, there was no way Amy had intended to be gone for long given that she hadn't even been wearing her shoes.

When Amy's parents couldn't locate her, they begged the ship's purser to search the ship and make an announcement. Also they requested Amy's photo be shown around to guests to ask if anyone had seen her. By lunchtime, the ship's captain told the Bradleys that he would not make an announcement that Amy was missing or post a picture for passengers to view for fear of "disturbing the guests." He assured the Bradleys that every inch of the ship had been searched.

The following day, with Amy still missing, Amy's parents left the ship to contact authorities. That day, they were informed by the F.B.I. that the only sections of the ship that had been checked were the common areas and restrooms.

On Thursday, March 26, Amy's mother, father and brother flew from Curacao to St. Maarten where they re-boarded the *Rhapsody of the Seas* and demanded a meeting with both the ship's captain and chief of security. Instead, they were greeted by a member of Royal Caribbean's 'risk management' team, who they later learned was an attorney assigned to represent the cruise line's interests against the Bradley family.

To date, according to Amy's mother, Royal Caribbean has failed to cooperate with the Bradley family in their search for answers to Amy's disappearance aboard their ship.

The day before leaving for vacation, Amy Lynn Bradley adopted a female bulldog named "Daisy." She had just moved into a new apartment and was starting a brand new job the week after the cruise. As her many friends and family have continued to express, there is no reason to believe Amy was suicidal or unhappy with her life.

On April 6, 2011, sixty-three-year-old Jon Halford, a bookseller from Buckinghamshire, United Kingdom, vanished from the liner *Thomson Spirit* while on a week-long Egyptian cruise. Hours before he had last been seen drinking cocktails in the upper-deck bar around twelve thirty in the morning, Halford had sent a text message to his wife, Ruth, back home to let her know he would see her at the airport the following day.

As Ruth was on her way to pick Jon up from his flight, the phone rang. "The plane is in the air but your husband is not on it," a Thomson's agent flatly expressed. Somehow, Jon had gone missing from the ship without anyone realizing—all despite the many checkpoints one must cross when disembarking.

When questioned, passengers who had remembered talking to Jon Halford in the bar that evening claimed he was not drunk. In fact, they said he was in good spirits and looking forward to seeing his wife and three children.

"A search of the sea was carried out at the time, but nothing was found," added Ruth. "I am told there are sharks in the area. It is very painful to think about."

Just a month earlier, twenty-four-year-old Rebecca Coraim, who had been working as the youth activities coordinator aboard the *Disney Wonder* was reported missing at sea off the western coast of Mexico after failing to report for a scheduled shift.

At five forty-five that morning, as later witnessed by her parents on a section of grainy surveillance camera videotape, Rebecca picked up a phone in the hallway of the ship, dialed an on-board number and then talked briefly to someone on the ship. What her parents witnessed next stunned and shocked them. During the call Rebecca's body language showed she was very emotional. As she hung up the phone, Rebecca began to cry.

That was the last image seen of her. To this day, there have been no answers as to her fate.

Rama Forman, a forty-eight-year-old Swiss native living in North London vanished from Silversea's luxurious liner, the *Silver Cloud*, a small ship that carries only three hundred guests along with two hundred twenty-two crewmembers. By the time the ship docked in Mumbai, the final port of call for the voyage, Rama was discovered to be missing.

Suspicious was the fact that Rama's balcony room was found to have been locked from the inside. Though her purse was still there in the room, all the jewelry she had taken along with her on the trip was missing.

Just eight days before his thirty-seventh birthday, Christopher Caldwell was squeezing every last moment out of a three day Carnival Cruise to Mexico with his fiancée. Instead of going back to his room to pack on the last night of the trip, Chris ventured back to the ship's casino where onboard video surveillance cameras captured him staying until two seventeen a.m. Sometime around three thirty a.m. on July 23, 2004, a bartender spotted a very drunk Chris on the promenade deck. Instead of making sure Chris made it safely to his cabin, the bartender chose to ignore the inebriated passenger.

It is most probable that Christopher Caldwell fell overboard some fourteen miles southeast of the Cape Florida lighthouse. An exhaustive search was performed by the Coast Guard. After thirty-six hours had passed with no sign of his whereabouts, Chris was presumed dead.

On May 15, 2006, less than twenty-four hours after boarding the Royal Caribbean *Mariner of the Seas*, Daniel DiPiero awoke from an inebriated state on a deck chair around two fifteen a.m. On video he was seen walking to the railing where he apparently vomited before sliding over the rail into the sea.

Sixty-eight-year old John Dresp of Omaha, Nebraska, was a first-time snorkeler in the water of the Belize Barrier Reef. Along with his brother Don and Don's wife, Winifred, John boarded a catamaran operated by Discovery Divers after arriving in Caye Cauker aboard the Norwegian Cruise Line's *Norwegian Dream*. The current and conditions that day were far from ideal for a snorkel trip, especially for a novice like John. While another of the ship's contracted excursion companies pulled their guests out of the water after ten minutes, Discovery went about with their normal itinerary. At first, it was Don who had gotten into trouble, requiring a rescue from the guides after being pulled far from the boat by the current. When they returned, to Don's horror, John was now missing.

Thirteen months later, after traveling back to Belize City for a coroner's inquiry, Donald and Winifred Dresp spent a tearful hour in front of the Magistrate Court, reaffirming their previous testimony as to the events of John's disappearance. To their shock, no witnesses from Discovery Divers appeared in court due to the fact that they had never even received a summons. To make matters worse, the Dresps were forced to fire their attorney, Louis Young, who they claimed demanded six hundred dollars in cash in advance.

Later, the Dresps learned that local rumor had placed John alive and well in Europe, living off of insurance money received in the fraud. It was noted that two days after John's disappearance, five Belizian fishermen also vanished in the current, yet only the American was presumed to have faked his own death.

Sadly, a very common thread in nearly every single documented case of suspicious disappearances involving cruise ship passengers is what is often described as a climate of obstructionism and insensitivity by those handling such difficult investigations. The frustration felt by family members confronted with the loss of a loved one, along with the inability—and in some alleged circumstances, sheer incompetence—of the authorities in charge of finding the truth can be overwhelming.

Such is the case of the family of Angelo Faliva, a head chef aboard the Royal Caribbean *Coral Princess*. After Angelo's November 25, 2009 disappearance during the middle of his shift, his family, in particular his sister, Chiara, has been tirelessly fighting to obtain answers that have yet to come. According to an Italian newspaper, two months after Angelo's disappearance, Chiara received an email from Bermuda police notifying her that they had not yet examined the data on Angelo's laptop computer, camera, or three cell phones they had in custody because they were "very busy with other matters." They did, however, find time to warn Chiara that her family was "on the verge" of harassing the Bermuda police with their constant inquiries.

It should be noted the circumstances surrounding Angelo Faliva's case are rather curious. The day Angelo vanished, the *Coral Princess* was a mere two miles offshore of Cartagena, Columbia where it was set to dock the next morning at nine a.m. To some this may appear to be a seemingly innocuous piece of information until one considers that discovered inside of the missing chef's hat was the name "Capilla del Mar," the very same hotel in Cartagena that had been researched from Angelo's own computer the morning of his disappearance. In addition, just one day before, on November 24, Angelo sent an email to Chiara mentioning a recent dispute with his boss on the ship, a sous chef who had filed a formal complaint in the matter.

With its many restaurants, the "promenade" seventh deck of the *Coral Princess* is not only heavily trafficked by passengers and crew alike, but is also under constant surveillance from security cameras monitoring the entire area. Sometime around eight fifteen p.m., Angelo returned to his post in the kitchen of Sabatini's after being seen conversing with two passengers. Shortly thereafter, he was observed entering an "employee's only" elevator that descended into, among many other places, an area where trash was routinely discarded into the sea.

This was the last confirmed sighting of Angelo even though another crewmember claimed seeing the chef on deck the next morning, despite the fact Angelo had not slept in his cabin during the night in question.

According to Bermuda police, who did not even begin their investigation onboard the *Coral Princess* until ten days after Angelo's disappearance, a single life preserver was also missing from deck seven, though the standard-issue night illumination flares attached to it had been torn off and left nearby on the deck.

It would seem strange that someone voluntarily entering the water in the dead of night would leave behind these safety flares. Certainly nobody attempting suicide by jumping off a ship would do so with the aid of a life jacket.

Falvia's family has several chilling theories. Could it be that Angelo fell victim to foul play?

Possibly pushed into the sea from a clandestine below-deck location by a disgruntled co-worker? Or was Angelo Falvia just in the wrong place at the wrong time, witnessing something he shouldn't have seen? Other scenarios seem less likely. Is it possible Angelo was decoyed to a storage area, subdued, put in a crate and taken onshore while cargo and luggage was moved, similar to one hypothesis held in the disappearance of Amy Lynn Bradley years earlier?

The ongoing idea of foul play aboard a cruise ship becomes a chilling consideration in the case of Annette Mizener. On December 4, 2004, during the last night of a nine-day Mexican Riviera cruise aboard Carnival's *The Pride*, Annette's small black-beaded evening bag was found on a lower deck of the ship just outside an Internet cafe. The purse was discovered torn and beads had been strewn all over. Nearby, an overturned drink glass and scattered papers were found alongside a railing.

Also found near the purse were spots of blood.

Perhaps most curious of all is that the security camera covering that part of the deck was later found to have a ship's map deliberately taped over the lens.

Annette had been traveling with her parents and teenage daughter. After winning twice at bingo while on the cruise, Annette planned to test her fortune again. She told her parents she would meet them for the ship's ten p.m. match, saying she wanted to arrive early so she could make sure and get her lucky seat.

When Annette didn't show up, her father became concerned and went to look for her. He was told she had been seen in the casino around nine thirty. After having her paged, a crewmember discovered Annette's purse on deck and paged her again at ten past ten to give it back.

According to Carnival, crew aboard *The Pride* conducted a three-hour long search aboard the ship, finding nothing. It was then after two a.m. that the captain called the U.S. Coast Guard, who instructed the ship to turn around and search the chilly sixty-degree waters. During this time, Annette's daughter, parents and a couple of other passengers had to block the attempt by Pride crewmembers to "clean up" the crime scene before finally prevailing in having the area in question roped off.

Still, no photos of the crime scene were ever taken, not by Carnival's highly-trained security staff, not even later by the F.B.I.

For sixteen hours, the U.S. Coast Guard, along with a Navy ship and search aircraft, scanned over eight hundred square miles of ocean to no avail.

Within a couple of months of Annette's disappearance, her husband John, who at the time of the cruise had been at home tending to the couple's new business selling dietary supplements, became very frustrated with the FBI. At first, he says, they told him they suspected foul play, in part due to inconsistencies in a particular crewmember's responses during questioning by authorities. As a year slipped by, the FBI's crime lab had still not examined DNA evidence collected from the scene.

According to the family, there remains a single person of interest (POI) in the strange case of Annette's disappearance—a single man in his mid-thirties who has never been married and has no children. As his story goes, he was out on the deck smoking a cigarette when he found Annette's purse, coincidentally at the very same moment two security guards arrived and collected her handbag. The POI witnessed the security guards remove a large amount of cash from the purse before he left the scene to join his traveling companions.

The POI is on record as having made no less than six trips back to the scene of the crime between eleven p.m. and one a.m.

An unofficial investigation into the POI's background done by Cruise Bruise, an organization that tracks cruise ship crime, allegedly found a number of curious circumstantial events. Three years before Annette Mizener vanished without a trace from the deck of *The Pride* another woman had gone missing from the POI's hometown of approximately sixty-five thousand people. Also reported was a case of a missing woman from a town the POI had recently visited. Oddly enough, both victims were between thirty and forty years old, married, with blond-hair and blue eyes, just like Annette.

In 2006, a year and a half after Annette Mizener vanished, DNA test results and fingerprints obtained from the POI turned up negative. The FBI removed him from their list of suspects though, like nearly all similar cruise ship disappearances, the case remains open.

Ask family members of those who have gone missing or died during pleasure cruises and almost all speak of similar circumstances of obstructionism and blatant untruths that have been told to them in their search for answers. Perhaps it is the law itself that is to blame. The current 'Death On The High Seas Act' (DOHSA), a 1920s law enacted by the US Congress, and which is still in effect, has complicated jurisdictional issues surrounding foreign-registered ships owned and/or operated by foreign-registered companies, sailing in international waters, and crossing territories and borders of countries. DOHSA has continued to protect the cruise industry from being held accountable for the safety and security of its passengers.

Judging from the mysterious stories of those dozens of people who have gone missing never to be seen again, it is not unheard of to fall victim to a suspicious disappearance aboard a cruise ship anywhere in the world today. Even as I write this chapter, five people have gone missing from cruise ships in just the first sixty days of 2012. Of course, a great many of these cases may indeed be the result of suicide, but still it would be hard to dismiss every single missing person case aboard a cruise ship as the desperate act of one wanting to kill themselves. Nonetheless, there seems to be no slowing down the number of people vanishing from cruise ships and even more disturbing, few answers for those families who have reason to believe foul play may have somehow been involved.

WHAT HAPPENED ABOARD THE COSTA CONCORDIA?

Their website reads: *No matter what travel destinations you are considering, a cruise vacation is the best way to travel in comfort and style. Costa Cruises' vacation packages will take you to the most fascinating travel destinations in the world: Western and Eastern Mediterranean, Norwegian Fjords, Baltic, Western and Eastern Caribbean, Red and Arabic Sea, Atlantic, Pacific and Indian Ocean.*

Perhaps it wasn't the most well-known cruise ship in the world. No *Love Boat*, no Disney floating city. Maybe they should have sensed something back on September 2, 2005 when the champagne bottle failed to break during its christening. On Friday January 13, 2012, at around six thirty pm local time, the Costa *Concordia*, a massive five hundred seventy million dollar passenger liner more than three football fields long and weighing just about one hundred and fifteen tons, left the

Italian port of Civitavecchia on its way to sudden disaster.

Two and a half hours later, the ship would run around on a reef just one hundred and fifty meters off the shore of Isola del Giglio, capsizing and turning the Costa *Concordia* into the world's most notorious cruise ship in nearly a century since the Titanic met an iceberg it didn't like.

How did it all happen?

One could call it "user error," though it may be a good idea to talk to *Concordia's* captain Francesco Schettino first.

Born in 1960 near Naples in the coastal town of Castellammare di Stabia, then later attending a nautical institute in the nearby town of Piano di Sorrento, nearly all of Schettino's life had been influenced by the sea. In 2002, he became employed by Costa Cruises, first as an official in charge of security. Within four years time, he was promoted to the role of Captain after having moved up to the title of "second in command."

On the evening of January, 13, 2012, the seemingly cowardly Captain Schettino was caught abandoning the *Concordia* as the crippled ship lay listing on its starboard side, half submerged in water. From his lifeboat, Schettino refused orders to return to his ship to oversee the evacuation, insisting it was dark.

The following is an English-translated transcript of the radio conversation between Capt. Francesco Schettino, and Capt. Gregorio De Falco of the Italian Coast Guard in Livorno. Within hours of its release to the world, the Italian Coast Guard confirmed this transcript's authenticity to The Associated Press.

—De Falco: "This is De Falco speaking from Livorno. Am I speaking with the commander?"
—Schettino: "Yes. Good evening, Cmdr. De Falco."
—De Falco: "Please tell me your name."
—Schettino: "I'm Cmdr. Schettino, commander"
—De Falco: "Schettino? Listen Schettino. There are people trapped on board. Now you go with your boat under the prow on the starboard side. There is a pilot ladder. You will climb that ladder and go on board. You go on board and then you will tell me how many people there are. Is that clear? I'm recording this conversation, Cmdr. Schettino..."
—Schettino: "Commander, let me tell you one thing..."
—De Falco: "Speak up! Put your hand in front of the microphone and speak more loudly, is that clear?"
—Schettino: "In this moment, the boat is tipping..."
—De Falco: "I understand that, listen, there are people that are coming down the pilot ladder of the prow. You go up that pilot ladder, get on that ship and tell me how many people are still on board. And what they need. Is that clear? You need to tell me if there are children, women or people in need of assistance. And tell me the exact number of each of these categories. Is that clear? Listen Schettino, that you saved yourself from the sea, but I am going to...really do something bad to you...I am going to make you pay for this. Go on board, Christ!!"
—Schettino: "Commander, please..."
—De Falco: "No, please. You now get up and go on board. They are telling me that on board there are still..."
—Schettino: "I am here with the rescue boats, I am here, I am not going anywhere, I am here..."

—De Falco: "What are you doing, commander?"
—Schettino: "I am here to coordinate the rescue..."
—De Falco: "What are you coordinating there? Go on board! Coordinate the rescue from aboard the ship. Are you refusing?"
—Schettino: "No, I am not refusing."
—De Falco: "Are you refusing to go aboard commander? Can you tell me the reason why you are not going?"
—Schettino: "I am not going because the other lifeboat is stopped."
—De Falco: "You go aboard. It is an order. Don't make any more excuses. You have declared 'abandon ship.' Now I am in charge. You go on board! Is that clear? Do you hear me? Go, and call me when you are aboard. My air rescue crew is there."
—Schettino: "Where are your rescuers?"
—De Falco: "My air rescue is on the prow. Go. There are already bodies, Schettino."
—Schettino: "How many bodies are there?"
—De Falco: "I don't know. I have heard of one. You are the one who has to tell me how many there are. Christ."
—Schettino: "But do you realize it is dark and here we can't see anything..."
—De Falco: "And so what? You want go home, Schettino? It is dark and you want to go home? Get on that prow of the boat using the pilot ladder and tell me what can be done, how many people there are and what their needs are. Now!"
—Schettino: "...I am with my second in command."
—De Falco: "So both of you go up then ... You and your second go on board now. Is that clear?"
—Schettino: "Commander, I want to go on board, but it is simply that the other boat here ... there are other rescuers. It has stopped and is waiting..."

—De Falco: "It has been an hour that you have been telling me the same thing. Now, go on board. Go on board! And then tell me immediately how many people there are there."
—Schettino: "Okay, commander"
—De Falco: "Go, immediately!"

Costa Cruises chief executive Pier Luigi Foschi quickly issued a statement laying claim that the fatal disaster happened because Schettino deviated from the pre-programmed route that would have taken the *Concordia* a safe distance from Isola del Giglio. Italian prosecutors quickly ruled out "technical error" as the accident's cause. Eyewitness accounts firmly point to Schettino's poor choice to show off by maneuvering the *Concordia* too close to shore.

Corriere della Sera, an Italian daily newspaper published in Milan, ran a story on January 16 describing how Schettino had chosen to pass close to the shore to please the *Concordia's* head waiter, Antonello Tievoli, a native of Giglio. According to witnesses, Schettino summoned Mr. Tievoli up to the bridge saying, "Antonello, come see, we are very close to your Giglio."

As Tievoli watched, his response moments before the accident occurred was, "Careful, we are extremely close to the shore."

Schettino then sounded the ship's throaty horn in a salute to retired captain, Mario Palombo, with whom Schettino was on the phone with at the time. Giglio residents claim they had never witnessed the *Concordia* come so close to the "Le Scole" reef area before.

"This was too close, too close," moaned Italo Arienti, a 54-year-old sailor who for more than a decade has worked on the ferry that runs between Giglio and the mainland.

In the main dining room, the first course had just been served. Tables shook as wine glasses, silverware and dishes of finely sautéed cuttlefish and mushrooms smashed to the floor. The Costa *Concordia*, carrying four thousand two hundred people (approx. three thousand two hundred passengers and one thousand crew members) crashed into a jagged reef hidden meters below the surface of the water, ripping a one hundred sixty-foot long gash in its hull before turning on its side.

Inside the ship, panic ensued. Hallways turned sideways and went dark as the electrical lights flickered to black.

In what can only be described as the height of irony, one passenger, a Swiss native named Yannick Sgaga, claimed that in the moments before the fateful crash, playing over the loudspeakers inside one of the *Concordia's* many lounges was Celine Dion's "My Heart will Go On," otherwise known as the theme from the movie "Titanic."

Despite the panic on board and the obvious mutiny by some of the junior crew who were well aware of the situation, Schettino did not make the call to "abandon ship" until an hour after the crash. This inexplicable delay made lifeboat rescue eventually impossible for some of the passengers, many of who jumped into the sea while others waited for helicopters to pluck them to safety.

Less than seventy-two hours after the accident, Captain Schettino was in custody in Grosseto prison, accused not only of multiple manslaughter charges, but also for abandoning his passengers on the ship. In a closed-door hearing, a defiant Schettino fervently dismissed all allegations that he abandoned the *Concordia*. "I saved the lives of hundreds, thousands of people. After the collision with the rocks the ship listed ninety degrees. I could not get back on board.

"The passengers were pouring on to the decks, taking the lifeboats by assault. I didn't even have a life jacket because I had given it to one of the passengers. I was trying to get people to get into the boats in an orderly fashion. Suddenly, since the ship was at a sixty to seventy degree angle, I tripped and I ended up in one of the boats. That's how I found myself in the lifeboat," claimed the captain.

"Suspended there, I was unable to lower the boat into the sea, because the space was blocked by other boats in the water."

Schettino did eventually admit responsibility for the crash. "I made a mistake on the approach," he said. "I was navigating by sight because I knew the depths well and I had done this maneuver three or four times. But this time I ordered the turn too late and I ended up in water that was too shallow. I don't know why it happened. I was a victim of my instincts."

On a Facebook page started in defense of Schettino, one man claiming to be a seasoned maritime expert noted that, despite allegations of the captain's ill-advised maneuver, Schettino's claim of having saved lives is quite accurate given the possibility things could have been much worse if he hadn't acted at all.

Perhaps none of his supporters were there to see Schettino wrapped in a blanket on his way to the Giglio shore around eleven thirty p.m., some four hours before evacuation of the *Concordia* was completed. According to one news report, Schettino quickly hailed a taxi, telling the driver, "Get me as far away from here as possible."

Later, when questioned by authorities, the taxi driver described Schettino as visibly shaken and inquiring where he could buy some dry socks.

There were also reports that shortly before the accident, Schettino was seen drinking in one of the ship's many bars with a beautiful blonde woman on his arm. This same woman, according to eyewitnesses, was on the bridge at the time of the crash. Even more outrageous is the puzzling story that immediately after the crash, Schettino ordered dinner for him and his female guest.

Five days after the accident, divers used explosives to blow a hole in the *Concordia's* hull in an attempt to find those that remained missing. Five bodies were found.

The first of the dead to be identified was thirty-eight-year-old Hungarian violinist, Sandor Feher, an entertainer on the ship. Jozsef Balog, a pianist working with Feher on the *Concordia*, told a local newspaper that Feher had helped put lifejackets on several crying children before making the fateful decision to return to his cabin to pack his violin instead of boarding a lifeboat without his precious instrument.

In the days after the *Concordia* disaster, Carnival Corporation of Miami, the parent company of Costa Cruises, saw shares of their stock drop more than sixteen percent in London amid questions regarding the safety of their ships. However, analysts were quick to claim that although the overall effect of the fatal Costa *Concordia* shipwreck may hurt the cruise industry in the short run, it would not have long-term negative effects.

"When a plane crashes, people don't stop flying," one analyst was anonymously quoted.

A week after the fatal crash, Costa Cruises offered *Concordia* passengers a thirty percent discount on future cruises. Unsurprisingly, what the attempted settlement achieved was anger from the survivors and unanimous scorn from the global media.

Days later, Costa upped their offer to eleven thousand euros, approximately fourteen thousand four hundred sixty U.S. dollars, as compensation, presumably for the loss of belongings and any psychological trauma the passengers may have suffered from being aboard a ship that capsized and nearly killed them. In addition, all passengers would be reimbursed for the full cost of their trip aboard the *Concordia* as well as any return travel expenses and medical expenses incurred due to the disaster.

Again, unsurprisingly, this offer, which one would assume would include provisions to drop any further legal action as well as sign lengthy nondisclosure agreements, generated more unfavorable media coverage and refusal by many passengers to sign the deal.

In the wake of the *Concordia's* unfortunate and avoidable disaster, consumer groups have begun to engage top U.S. law firms with the aim of filing a massive class-action suit against Costa's parent company, Miami-based Carnival Cruises. Their expectation is that they will force Costa and Carnival to cough up a settlement in the range of anywhere between two hundred thousand to one and a half million dollars per uninjured passenger. For some, including angry sixty-two-year-old German passenger Herbert Greszuk, who left behind everything in the crash, including his dentures, it's a matter of forcing Costa to be accountable and to make sure something like this never happens again.

However, in the end, it may be the fine print on the tickets purchased and signed by the *Concordia's* passengers that decides how much, if any, Costa will have to pay out. Inside the ticket contract is what is commonly known as a "choice of forum" clause that clearly states lawsuits must be filed in Genoa, Italy where most of Costa Cruise's operations are based. If a Costa cruise were to touch any part of U.S. territory, the suit would have to be filed in Miami, but the *Concordia* only ever traveled in foreign waters during this journey. Since Italian law makes it more difficult for some plaintiffs to recover damages due to pain and suffering, the pursuit of legal remedies may be a very uphill battle for the injured and non-injured *Concordia* passengers alike.

Also, what is to become of the *Concordia's* one thousand crew members who not only suffered through the disaster but are now out of work? For them, legal options are quite limited given how their employment contracts require them to first submit to arbitration before any lawsuits can be brought.

Is there any question that this was a tragedy that could have been avoided? One of the most stunning pieces of information to come from the investigation is the revelation that this was not the first time Francesco Schettino had crashed a cruise ship. In June 2010, Schettino maneuvered the *Aida Blu* into the German port of Warnemunde too quickly, causing damage to the ship.

As the *Concordia* hearings began, documents surfaced containing claims that officers aboard the Costa *Concordia* were seen snorting cocaine and getting drunk on a regular basis. It's not impossible to see why this alleged hard-partying atmosphere on the ship has been mentioned as a mitigating cause of a disaster that should never have happened.

Thirty two people lost their lives on the *Concordia*.

MEXICODE RED

Ah, Mexico. Sun and fun south of the border style, where you get lots of bang for your buck and the tequila flows like every day is Cinco de Mayo. Thousands of miles of beaches make it a tan-seeker's paradise. A certain amount of lax attitude gives it a nice cachet as a place where all types of whims and desires can be indulged depending upon how badly one wants to seek them out. Lots of people love to vacation in Mexico. Tons swear by it.

However, the prevailing question that seems to come back around in the media every couple of years or so is whether or not vacationing in Mexico is safe.

In case you haven't heard, or have been spending a lot of time in a cave, Mexico is home to one of the most brutal drug wars in modern history. Since 2006, the entire country has been gripped by fear, caught in the crosshairs of a horrifying escalation of extreme violence brought on by the government's attempted crackdown on renegade cartels that push enormous amounts of narcotics into the U.S. and abroad. It is the brutality and bloodshed from these narco wars that make the headlines. A dozen young men found massacred in a field, their bodies hacked to pieces. Rival gang members or snitches found hanging from bridges in densely populated areas. The bloody photos of victims published in tabloids there, yet rarely seen in the United States, are nothing short of barbaric. Forty-five thousand Mexican troops have been enlisted into this seemingly unwinnable war to stop this multi-billion dollar illicit industry. Still the dead pile up like kindling.

In April 2011 alone, the death toll from the narco wars topped fourteen hundred—a seeming drop in the bucket compared to the tens of thousands who have found themselves caught in the crossfire. Google it and you will find a hundred news stories full of kidnapping, beheadings and torture so gruesome they make the movie "Scarface" look like an episode of "Mickey Mouse Clubhouse."

On February 8 2012, the U.S. Department of State issued the following updated travel advisory:

Millions of U.S. citizens safely visit Mexico each year for study, tourism, and business, including more than 150,000 who cross the border every day. The Mexican government makes a considerable effort to protect U.S. citizens and other visitors to major tourist destinations, and there is no evidence that Transnational Criminal Organizations (TCOs) have targeted U.S. visitors and residents based on their nationality. Resort areas and tourist destinations in Mexico generally do not see the levels of drug-related violence and crime reported in the border region and in areas along major trafficking routes.

Nevertheless, U.S. travelers should be aware that the Mexican government has been engaged in an extensive effort to counter TCOs which engage in narcotics trafficking and other unlawful activities throughout Mexico. The TCOs themselves are engaged in a violent struggle to control drug trafficking routes and other criminal activity. As a result, crime and violence are serious problems throughout the country and can occur anywhere. U.S. citizens have fallen victim to TCO activity, including homicide, gun battles, kidnapping, carjacking and highway robbery.

According to the most recent homicide figures published by the Mexican government, 47,515 people were killed in narcotics-related violence in Mexico between December 1, 2006 and September 30, 2011, with 12,903 narcotics-related homicides in the first nine months of 2011 alone. While most of those killed in narcotics-related violence have been members of TCOs, innocent persons have also been killed. The number of U.S. citizens reported to the Department of State as murdered in Mexico increased from 35 in 2007 to 120 in 2011.

Gun battles between rival TCOs or with Mexican authorities have taken place in towns and cities in many parts of Mexico, especially in the border region. Gun battles have occurred in broad daylight on streets and in other public venues, such as restaurants and clubs. During some of these incidents, U.S. citizens have been trapped and temporarily prevented from leaving the area. TCOs use stolen cars and trucks to create roadblocks on major thoroughfares, preventing the military and police from responding to criminal activity. The location and timing of future armed engagements is unpredictable. We recommend that you defer travel to the areas indicated in this Travel Warning and to exercise extreme caution when traveling throughout the northern border region.

The rising number of kidnappings and disappearances throughout Mexico is of particular concern. Both local and expatriate communities have been victimized. In addition, local police have been implicated in some of these incidents. We strongly advise you to lower your profile and avoid displaying any evidence of wealth that might draw attention.

Carjacking and highway robbery are serious problems in many parts of the border region and U.S. citizens have been murdered in such incidents. Most victims who complied with carjackers at these checkpoints have reported that they were not physically harmed. Incidents have occurred during the day and at night, and carjackers have used a variety of techniques, including bumping/moving vehicles to force them to stop and running vehicles off the road at high speeds. There are some indications that criminals have particularly targeted newer and larger vehicles, especially dark-colored SUVs. However, victims driving a variety of vehicles, from late model SUVs to old sedans have also been targeted. While violent incidents have occurred at all hours of the day and night on both modern toll ("cuotas") highways and on secondary roads, they have occurred most frequently at night and on isolated roads. To reduce risk, we strongly urge you to travel between cities throughout Mexico only during daylight hours, to avoid isolated roads, and to use toll roads whenever possible. The Mexican government has deployed federal police and military personnel throughout the country as part of its efforts to combat the TCOs. U.S. citizens traveling on Mexican roads and highways may encounter government checkpoints, which are often staffed by military personnel or law enforcement personnel. TCOs have erected their own unauthorized checkpoints, and killed or abducted motorists who have failed to stop at them. You should cooperate at all checkpoints.

Effective July 15, 2010, the U.S. Mission in Mexico imposed restrictions on U.S. government employees' travel. U.S. government employees and their families are not permitted to drive for personal reasons from the U.S.-Mexico border to or from the interior of Mexico or Central America. Personal travel by vehicle is permitted between Hermosillo and Nogales but is restricted to daylight hours and the Highway 15 toll road (cuota).

U.S. government personnel and their families are prohibited from personal travel to all areas described as "defer non-essential travel" and when travel for official purposes is essential it is conducted with extensive security precautions. USG personnel and their families are allowed to travel for personal reasons to the areas where no advisory is in effect or where the advisory is to exercise caution.

For more information on road safety and crime along Mexico's roadways, see the Department of State's Country Specific Information.

It's no secret that any kind of governmental communiqué to the public, especially those concerning anything as delicate as a travel advisory, is crafted first and foremost not to inspire panic amongst those who they are attempting to advise. The implication that there is any kind of "spin" put on the facts in order to make them seem palatable, not only to the general public, but also to the government and people of Mexico with whom the United States depends upon for trade and commerce, is only suggested because regardless of how much any of us would like to truly believe governments have our best interests at heart, these advisories are still a function of public relations.

That being said, there is one sentence in the very beginning of this travel advisory that bears closer inspection.

"...there is no evidence that Transnational Criminal Organizations (TCOs) have targeted U.S. visitors and residents based on their nationality."

Read it again. It doesn't say that TCO's have *not* targeted visitors; it only says they haven't targeted visitors *based on their nationality*.

It's a small, yet very crucial distinction, especially in light of the sections of the memo that clearly mention things like how carjacking in the border regions have resulted in U.S. citizens being murdered and also how you, as a visitor, should lower your profile as to not be noticed by the wrong elements.

Of course, it would be ridiculous to say the entire country of Mexico is a war zone and should be avoided because you may catch a stray bullet or be shot dead in a carjacking. However, according to the U.S. State Department's own travel advisory, places in Mexico to "defer non-essential travel" to include: "the northern state of Baja California, particularly at night;" "the state of Chihuahua;" "the state of Coahuila;" "the state of Durango;" "the state of Nuevo Leon, except the metropolitan area of Monterrey where you should exercise caution;" "the state of San Luis Potosi, except the city of San Luis Potosi where you should exercise caution;" "the state of Sinaloa except the city of Mazatlan where you should exercise caution particularly late at night and in the early morning;" "the eastern edge of the State of Sonora;" "the coastal town of Puerto Peñasco;" "the state of Tamaulipas;" "the state of Zacatecas except the city of Zacatecas where you should exercise caution;" "the areas of [Aguascalientes] that border the state of Zacatecas;" "the areas of the state of Colima that border the state of Michoacán;" "the area west and south of the town of Arcelia on the border with Estado de Mexico in the north and the town of Tlapa near the border with Oaxaca;" "areas of [Jalisco] that border the states of Michoacán and Zacatecas;" "the state of Michoacán except the cities of Morelia and Lázaro Cardenas where you should exercise caution;" "the state of Morelos;" "the state of Nayarit north of the city of Tepic as well as to the cities of Tepic and Xalisco;" and "the state of Veracruz."

For those of you keeping score at home, that equates to fourteen out of the thirty Mexican states.

And though nearly all of this incredible violence tends to take place in urban centers rife with the kind of low-income conditions that visitors' guides and brochures ignore, there have indeed been incidents where the fingers of this evil have touched the more resort-oriented areas as well. In January of 2011, fifteen headless bodies were found dumped in Acapulco. A sixteenth corpse was found in a nearby car, shot to death. Later, in September of the same year, five severed heads were found in a bag that had been left near a primary school in the resort city. Once the sun-drenched playground of the rich and famous like John F. Kennedy, John Wayne and Cary Grant, Acapulco has become embroiled in a turf war by gangs involved in the narco trade.

Though these bodies were all discovered in parts of the city off the beaten tourist path, in the same week those sixteen young men were found dead, two police officers were gunned down on a popular tourist strip along the Bahia de Acapulco.

By the end of 2011, the death toll in Acapulco alone had reached nearly nine hundred in a country where the drug war had claimed a record fifteen thousand two hundred seventy-three lives. The picturesque beaches and hotels where countless visitors had come for decades to forget their troubles, is now a playground of fear.

It's easy to simplify the reasons why tourism to Acapulco has dropped dramatically over the last few years. Whether you want to point to any sort of combination of a flagging global economy and jitters over the unrelenting violence in the streets, hotel occupancy rates have reportedly dropped to historic lows in Acapulco.

Sadly though, it is not only those connected with the drug trade that end up victims of this barbarism. In November of 2010, eighteen residents of nearby Michoacán were abducted and later found in a mass grave. The men, most of them related, had been part of a group of mechanics who saved their money each year in order to take an annual vacation in Acapulco together. Later, a drug baron named Carlos Montemayor, known on the streets as "Barbie," claimed the mechanics had been mistaken for members of a rival cartel.

Oops.

However, it seems that Acapulco's loss has become Cancun's gain as visitors continue to flock to its golden beaches. Realizing its shaky hold as the number one vacation destination in the Caribbean was at great risk, local officials have made a priority of stepping up security in the tourist zone. Now, because Americans make up such a large number of the nearly six million international visitors to Cancun, they have even made it so help can be accessed by dialing the very familiar 911 from any working telephone.

As far as anyone can tell, not a single Cancun tourist has been killed in narco-cartel related violence.

That is not to say that American tourists haven't died in Mexico from highly suspicious circumstances.

In January 6, 2007, twenty-two-year old Nolan Webster from Woburn, Massachusetts, arrived in Cancun on what was supposed to be a one-week dream vacation with his girlfriend, Kristen. The trip had been a college graduation gift from his parents purchased from a company called Apple Vacations. Nolan and Kristen's room was booked at the all-inclusive Oasis Hotel, an upscale resort that boasts eighteen restaurants, eighteen bars, six hundred fifty meters of beachfront and a three hundred meter swimming pool touted on their website as being the longest in Latin America.

Less than thirty hours after arriving in Cancun, Nolan Webster alive, but unconscious, was pulled from that very same four-and-a-half-foot deep pool. It is what happened afterwards that is truly disturbing.

Below is a first person account of the incident:

On the seventh day of January 2007, at approximately four p.m., I was walking along the poolside with my wife. I observed a male pulling a second male (victim) from the floor of the pool. At first I thought that it was some type of event or joke, but quickly realized that it was an emergency situation.

I ran to the edge of the pool where I met the male with the victim. I grabbed onto the victim with both hands and pulled him out of the pool. I laid the victim onto his back and checked his vital signs. I was unable to locate a pulse on the victim and the victim had no signs of breathing. I observed a purple-ish substance coming from the victim's mouth. There appeared to be blood running from his nose as well.

I attempted to arouse the victim by touching his face and arms. There was no response. I then stood up above the victim and screamed for help. I yelled approximately ten times asking for someone to help. Screaming first that I needed a doctor, nurse or paramedic, I then yelled for anyone who knew CPR.

A young male in his twenties was standing next to me. This male stated that he did not know CPR, but was willing to assist. I knelt beside the victim and started clearing out his mouth attempting to remove any obstruction from his airway. After clearing the airway, I started CPR compressions. As I was compressing, just more of the (purple-ish) substance was exiting his mouth. Again I cleared the airway. I returned to the chest area and once again commenced chest compressions. This continued for approximately ten minutes. Every few minutes I stood up and screamed for help. At one point, I observed the victim make gurgling noises and believed that he was becoming responsive. However, once I stopped the compressions the noises stopped as well. There were a few times during the resting phase of compressions that the victim appeared to have sucked back a breath. At this point I stopped the compressions to see if the victim was responding. When the victim remained VSA (Vital Signs Absent) I continued the compressions.

I observed a male dive into the pool from the opposite side and swim to our location. This male identified himself as a member of the U.S. Military Reserves and stated that he knew CPR. Again, I started chest compressions and he assisted with mouth-to-mouth rescue breathing. This continued for approximately ten more minutes.

I then observed a male lifeguard running from the beach direction. I had observed a lifeguard several times on the beach the past few days, "rescuing" people who swam out too far and were in danger of not being able to make it back to shore. The lifeguard ran across the pool bar and stopped just short of our location. I looked at him and he just shrugged his shoulders as if he didn't know what to do.

At this time a female arrived who stated she had some type of medical background and knelt down beside the victim. I then moved away from the chest area to allow her to take over CPR. At approximately the same time, another male arrived who stated that he was a trauma room nurse and he too knelt beside the victim to assist. I then stood up and watched their attempts to rescue the victim.

I observed a male who appeared to be a doctor (as he was wearing a long white coat and had a stethoscope around his neck) standing at the pool and looking at the victim. He did not attempt to assist in the rescue. I stood off to the side away from the victim and rescuers.

Approximately five minutes after I stepped away, I observed two paramedics running toward the victim. They were carrying equipment bags and what appeared to be an oxygen tank. The paramedics leaned over the victim and checked his vital signs, pulled a white sheet from one of their bags and placed it over the victim. I heard the male, who stated that he was a nurse, argue with the paramedics asking for them to help the victim. I heard someone say that the victim needed compressed oxygen and that he was willing to give it to him, but the paramedics refused access to the oxygen bottle. I observed a short struggle over the equipment bags between the assisting witness and the paramedics.

I was shocked that the man who appeared to be the resort doctor did not attempt to assist in the rescue of the victim. I simply could not believe that the paramedics made no attempts to revive the victim at any point. The entire time that this event was occurring, a pool bartender at the resort just stood by and watched. He made no attempts to call for help or to assist.

After a short time, a female arrived at the location. She appeared to be a staff member of the resort as she carried a handheld radio and was adorned with a resort identification badge. She was informing people to stay away from the victim and telling everyone to move back. Everyone who was assisting was told to move away from the victim. My wife and I remained on scene for approximately twenty minutes after being told to leave. I asked the female if she required my information, stating that I assisted in attempting to rescue the victim. She said no and asked that I just leave the area. I observed the staff place plastic pool chairs around the victim as he lay on the deck beside the pool.

My wife and I left the scene and returned or rooms. I still do not believe what just occurred. I've been a police officer in Canada for ten years and have seen many deaths, but never have I seen such a poor attempt by medical staff (Doctor/Paramedics) to assist a person in need of medical treatment.

We returned to the scene approximately two hours later and observed that the victim was still lying near the side of the pool. Another two hours went by and we returned to the scene and I couldn't believe that the victim was still lying there.

Sadly, the tragic disregard for Nolan Webster's being didn't end there. According to chilling details posted by Nolan's mother, Maureen Webster, on her own website, MexicoVacationAwareness.com, Nolan's girlfriend Kristen phoned her in hysterics, saying, "I think Nolan's dead!" It would be the only call Nolan's family would receive from anyone to inform them of what had happened to their son.

And if the first-hand account depicting the resort staff's total apathy during Nolan's rescue wasn't horrifying enough, the final unspeakable injustice happened when his father made the solemn trip to Cancun to recover Nolan's body only to discover the Oasis Hotel had charged Nolan for his night's stay.

It would be easy to dismiss the allegedly questionable actions of the rescue and medical personnel in this one case as an isolated singular event—an anomaly. However, Nolan Webster's senseless death is not the only incident over the past few years that calls into question the quality of emergency medical care afforded to tourists in Mexico.

In what can only be described as tragic irony, exactly five years after Nolan Webster died due to what could be easily categorized as lack of proper care, thirty-year old Joseph Bitet, a former Marine turned Army Reservist who had completed two tours of Iraq and was about to be deployed to Kuwait, met his fate in Cancun on January 7, 2012.

Joseph and his girlfriend, Allyson Jo Paria, were staying at the Riu Cancun Resort. She had returned to the room while Joseph remained at the bar at the neighboring Riu Las Americas, texting and calling Allyson from time to time. At four minutes past three a.m. Joseph sent a text saying he was on his way back up to their room.

But he never arrived. Instead, she received a phone call from the front desk telling her to come to the lobby because Joseph was hurt. She rushed down just in time to see him on a stretcher being placed in an ambulance.

According to hotel officials, Joseph Bitet had fallen five stories from a window to the concrete below.

Joseph was alive, but seriously injured. What happened next was not uncommon. The Cancun hospital Joseph was taken to demanded thousands of dollars upfront before they would even treat him. Allyson allowed them to charge six thousand dollars to her credit card.

Sadly, Joseph Bitet soon died from his injuries. Allyson was then told he had a collapsed lung and had gone into cardiac arrest. When his parents arrived hours later, they asked to see the room where Joseph had been treated and instantly noticed there was no medical equipment in sight.

It was at this point that the hospital demanded an additional three thousand four hundred dollars from Joseph's family. His parents argued, trying to tell the hospital staff that their son had his own insurance. However, the hospital refused to let them leave, even placing two security guards nearby to make sure they couldn't exit the building until the payment was made.

In the wake of trying to determine exactly what could have caused Joseph's injuries, the police refused to help, initially saying that Joseph's death was accidental. They said he had somehow climbed up on the roof alone. The security camera tapes told a much different story. After much persuasion, Joseph's family was allowed to view the footage. On camera, Joseph leaves the bar at three fifteen. Five minutes later, he was seen speaking to a mysterious unidentified male for a few minutes, then obtaining a light for a cigarette from someone dressed in the uniform of hotel personnel. At three twenty-three, Joseph boarded the elevator with this mystery man.

Seven minutes later, a Russian man emerged from the elevator yelling that his wife had just seen a man fall from the fifth floor.

During the cursory investigation, the Russian couple, who were staying in Room 238, were never questioned by police. The mystery man who entered the elevator with Joseph Bitet, perhaps the last person to see him alive, was never identified. The case remains unsolved to this day.

On June 21, 2006, sixteen-year old Andrew Smith, described by his family as a fun-loving kid who loved to play high school football, was waiting for the elevator on the fourth floor of the Hotel Solaris. Remarking that the elevator was taking a long time, Andrew then unsuspectingly leaned against a painted white plywood structure, which to the surprise of those around him, hinged inward toward an open elevator shaft. As the unsecured and unmarked barrier collapsed under Andrew's weight, the boy plunged five stories into the hotel's basement.

When his family looked down into the darkness, they were stunned to discover Andrew was now impaled through his torso on a metal rod.

Fifteen crucial minutes passed before the ambulance arrived. Paramedics quickly administered oxygen and an I.V., however they told Andrew's parents that they weren't authorized to move the boy until a doctor arrived. Thirty-five minutes later, it was a pediatrician not trained in trauma which showed up. He decided that the two hundred twenty-five pound Andrew was to be removed from the steel shaft thrust through his abdomen instead of cutting the metal rod away. By the time they got Andrew onto a stretcher, part of the boy's intestines hung outside of his body and he was bleeding out.

In the ambulance, Andrew's father had to hold onto the gurney to keep it from rolling around because it wasn't strapped down. During the entire ride, the pediatrician did nothing to stop the bleeding. He didn't even speak one word to Andrew even as the boy kept pleading for, "Aqua… aqua…"

Andrew arrived at the Las Americas Hospital alive but fading fast. Despite being told an operating room would be ready when they got there, Andrew was left waiting in a corridor while nurses unwrapped medical equipment and began spraying it down. It was twenty minutes later that doctors came to Andrew's parents in the waiting room to tell them their son's heart had stopped several times on the table before eventually giving out for the last time.

The day after Andrew bled to death, his aunt was exchanging money at the front desk of the Hotel Solaris when she overheard another guest ask the manager about how the boy in the elevator was doing. Without missing a beat, the manager told the unsuspecting guest, "He's just fine. He didn't even break a bone." A local Cancun newspaper printed that Andrew died after jumping from a balcony at the hotel.

That morning, the Las Americas Hospital called Andrew's parents demanding payment and threatened that the family would not be allowed to leave Mexico until the bill was paid.

Unsurprisingly, when it comes to Americans who die unexpectedly in Mexico, there are also unscrupulous dirtbags working to con grieving families out of money by playing on their fragile emotions and severe vulnerability. Davon Green-Franklin was a twenty-two-year old bright Howard University senior visiting Cancun on his final spring break before he was set to graduate. On March 13, 2010 Davon tweeted eighteen times back and forth with friends. One of which read: *Looking for someone to daydream with.. we will dream of life until life becomes a dream...*

In another ominously prescient message, Davon tweeted: *Life Lessons from the ocean water: the waves will pull you out further before they take you back to shore.*

One day later, Davon Green-Franklin's leg cramped up while he was swimming in the ocean. Davon, a trained swimmer and promising athlete, struggled and called for help. By the time his friends pulled him to shore, Davon had stopped breathing. At Amerimed Hospital in Cancun, he was pronounced dead.

A mere half hour after Davon's girlfriend called Inez and Chavez Franklin, to tell them of the tragic news of their son, their phone rang again. This time it was a man identifying himself as "Jesus" who claimed he worked at the resort where Davon had been staying. Jesus told the distraught Franklins that they needed to give him a credit card number to cover Davon's ambulance and hospital bills.

Instantly, Inez knew something sounded amiss. Why, she wondered, would someone from the hotel be handling such a thing? The explanation Jesus gave was sketchy. Again, he demanded a credit card number. Inez refused and hung up.

Minutes later, she received a second call. This time from a man with the same voice, but now claiming he was calling from the hospital's billing department. Again, Inez hung up without giving the man a credit card number. Disgustingly enough, it was quite obvious to her that someone in Mexico was attempting to take advantage of them in their time of grief.

Soon thereafter, the Franklins were shocked to discover that Davon, while still injured, had been refused transport in a Mexican ambulance until his friends who were with him could come up with six hundred dollars in cash.

Yet, perhaps the most heart-wrenching story of all is that of the tragically stolen life of eight-year old Brent Midlocks.

As with any family vacation, the Midlocks had hoped for memories to last a lifetime. Instead, they left Mexico amidst a gruesome nightmare. When they arrived in Mexico, they discovered their original hotel had been overbooked and they had been moved to the nearby Occidental Grand Xcaret—an upscale, "family-friendly" seaside resort in Playa del Carmen on the Riviera Maya south of Cancun that featured a four-foot deep salt water pool promoted as a place to snorkel.

At eleven thirty a.m. on the morning of April 26, 2003, Brent Midlocks and his sisters, all accomplished swimmers and members of local swim teams back home in Shorewood, Illinois, entered the man-made snorkeling lagoon. After twenty minutes, Brent's mother, Nancy ordered some beverages from a poolside waiter. She asked her eldest daughter, Jana, to get her two younger siblings out of the water.

Moments later, Jana came to her mother, panicked. Brent was nowhere to be found. Frantic, Nancy began searching around the lagoon. At the pool's bottom, she discovered one of his swim fins. His snorkel was discovered four hundred feet away.

Still there was no sign of the boy.

Quickly, they began calling out Brent's name. Within two hours, Amber Alert posters had been placed around the resort. Resort officials allegedly told the Midlocks over and over that they had no information while continuing to imply that Brent was missing.

It would be eighteen hours until the horrifying truth about what had happened to Brent Midlocks would be revealed to his family.

In the dead of night, Brent's lifeless and battered body was recovered from deep inside one of the snorkeling lagoon's underwater drains. The twelve inch diameter pipe sucked water from the pool at a bone crushing six hundred psi—strong enough to have pulled in Brent's eighty-five-pound body in less than a second, folding him in half and dislocating his shoulders, right elbow and left knee.

During the search of the pool, The Midlocks were forcibly kept away by resort staffers. At one point, a frantic Nancy Midlocks found herself staring straight into the barrel of an AK-47 assault rifle pointed directly at her face.

According to her later account, there was no lifeguard and no warning signs. There had been no reason at all to believe this serene pool hid a terrifying and deadly danger that would so tragically claim the life of an innocent eight-year-old boy.

Despite the terrifying drug war that continues to rage unabated, the Secretaria de Tourismo, Mexico's tourism agency, announced that in 2011, foreign travelers arriving by air increased to a record twenty two point seven million, the most since Bank of Mexico began tracking these statistics in 1980.

Tourism is one of Mexico's top sources of income.

While incidents resulting in the deaths of visitors to Mexico are not often as widely-reported as one may think, it was a close-call in February of 2012 that splashed the international news wires. Twenty-two unlucky passengers from the Carnival *Splendor* cruise ship were on a jungle excursion near Puerto Vallarta when a masked man robbed them of their valuables at gunpoint. According to passenger Kate Berry-Shoefsengers, a bandit wearing a bandana over his face and brandishing a gun stepped out in front of a narrow path as the tourists approached. In Spanish he demanded they put all their possessions on the ground, turn around and run. It's impossible to speculate whether any of the unlucky victims were in mortal danger; however they should all feel fortunate to have had a translator along with them who understood the orders of an armed robber.

INTERVIEW WITH MAUREEN WEBSTER

In 2007, Maureen's son, Nolan Webster died tragically while on a dream vacation in Cancun, Mexico after he was denied proper medical care.

What was it like getting that phone call?

I believe that we are all just one phone call away from being brought to our knees. Just like a tornado sucks the air out of a home, the phone call sucked the life out of my body. I fell to my knees and screamed. To this day, I don't know what words I was screaming. My life as I knew it was over. I would never be "whole" again. That phone call was the end of my "perfect" world and the beginning of a nightmare with no end.

Nolan had just graduated college before his trip. If he had never gone to Mexico, what do you think he'd be doing with his life today?

Nolan Webster never had a bad day in his life. At his wake, after viewing his body in the casket, one of his friends said, "that is the first time I ever saw Nolan without a smile." Nolan would be married to Kristen (the love of his life), have one or two children and a successful career. And he would definitely be smiling.

Your website, MexicoVacationAwareness.com chronicles several tragic Mexico vacation stories like Nolan's and Brent Midlock's. In addition, you also have published several messages and emails submitted by literally dozens of others who have lost their friends and loved ones in Mexico as well over just the last few years. What do you see as a common issue among the many incidents people have reported to you?

There are a couple of common issues in the incidents people have reported to me. The most common issue is that in almost every case, the "victim" was alone at the time of their death. The second most common issue is almost every family that I have come in contact with, does not believe what they are being told by the Mexican resort officials. They all feel that they are being lied to and that there is a lot more to the story. We were lied to about the circumstances surrounding Nolan's death and I believe that these other families are being lied to as well.

I was stunned to learn, very much after the fact, not only of Nolan's tragic and senseless death, but also of the shocking details of other deaths of those visiting Mexico. Why do you think these stories don't seem to get more coverage in the U.S.?

I think that most of these tragic stories receive local media attention and most people think that these tragedies are unique. The problem is that there are far too many local stories. If the media could somehow get these stories to a national level, the world would find out these tragedies are happening way too often. Since Nolan's tragic death, over twelve hundred U.S. citizens have died from a "non-natural" cause in Mexico. That is over thirty-two percent of *all* non-natural deaths outside this country! One of the main goals of my website is to have a central place to collect these stories so that people could clearly see what is happening in Mexico.

What, in your opinion, should be done and isn't being done to prevent tragedies such as Nolan's?

For the past five years I have been working with my Congressman Edward Markey. As a result of his efforts, the International Travelers Bill of Rights Act has been introduced into Congress. This bill will make it mandatory for a travel agent or tour operator to inform a consumer, in advance of their purchase, about any State Department issued travel warning or travel alerts to the country they are considering traveling to. How many consumers realize that Mexico is on the same State Department travel warning list as Iran, Iraq and Afghanistan? Why should the travel industry be exempt from attaching a warning label to the product that they are selling when every other industry in the U.S. is mandated to do so?

Because tourism is one of the largest industries in Mexico, one could argue that it seems like the incidents that result in serious accidents, violent crime and deaths of foreign visitors are sometimes marginalized in order to "protect" the jobs and livelihoods of people with very few or no other employment options. One could even say the primary interest of the employees is to keep the tourist money flowing without disruption, regardless of the impact those decisions have upon the visitors themselves or the cost of human lives. In a country with so much poverty, can conditions ever change?

Not only are these incidents "marginalized," they are completely ignored. Until the Mexican government and resort officials start accepting responsibility for many of these tragedies, nothing will ever change. They continue to place blame on the victim. Somehow, according to them, these victims caused or heavily contributed to their own death. More times than not, that is not the case. Mexico is a country full of poverty, but these resorts are often owned by multi-million dollar Spanish corporations. These corporations take full advantage of the lack of safety standards and enforcement in Mexico. They are pretty much "untouchable" and this totally unacceptable.

The U.S. Department of State has consistently issued travel advisories for Mexico. What else would you like to see them do in order to safeguard American citizens vacationing south of the border?

A lot of people don't realize that the U.S. government has no control when something happens to an American in Mexico. Even the U.S. Consulate is a "guest" in their country. Their hands are tied too. If you are in trouble in Mexico, you are basically on your own. There is no knight in shining armor that is going to be able to rescue you. I think our government needs to do more to make people aware of this fact. They need to do more to educate Americans. Perhaps with more education the number of people choosing to travel to Mexico would decline. This would force the travel industry to "self correct." The Mexican resorts would have to improve their safety standards in order to survive.

If you could share one message with other mothers out there, what would it be?

If there were five words in my entire life that I could take back, it would be these five words I said to Nolan…go to Mexico it's fun. Mexico is *not* fun. It is dangerous. Believe me you do not want to live a life like mine. Please learn from my mistake.

FLORIDA: THE GUNSHINE STATE

Florida: The land of sun-blasted fun, from the natural beauty of the Panhandle down to the art deco hotels and outdoor cafes of Miami Beach. Two thousand seven was a record year for tourism in Florida with more than eighty-four point five million visitors making the Sunshine State their destination of choice. Tourism generates well in excess of sixty billion dollars in revenue in the state of Florida and employs nearly one million people.

But is Florida safe?

It used to be that if you were a tourist in Florida, you were marked.

More accurately, your rental car was marked. Your license plate more than likely ended with a Y or a Z, a practice akin to putting a bull's-eye on your forehead, especially for criminals trolling for rental car plates coming out of Miami-Dade Airport in order to target unsuspecting tourists.

Uwe-Wilhelm Rakebrand, a thirty-three-year-old cultural engineer from Hamburg, Germany had just arrived on a belated honeymoon with his pregnant twenty-seven year-old wife. Shortly after twelve thirty a.m., they were headed east on State Road 836 toward their hotel in Miami Beach. Rakebrand's wife was in the passenger seat reading a German-language crime safety brochure when the red Toyota Corolla they had just picked up from Alamo mere minutes earlier was rammed from behind by a light-colored van.

Terrified, Rakebrand's wife implored her husband not to stop the car. As they tried to escape, the van rammed them again, continuing its pursuit. As the van then pulled alongside of the Toyota, a single shot was fired, fatally hitting Uwe-Wilhelm Rakebrand in the back as he lost control of his car.

Within hours, police had arrested nineteen-year-old high-school dropout Recondall (Rico) Wiggins for Rakebrand's murder. By morning, both the *New York Times* and *Los Angeles Times* ran photos of Rakerbrand's sheet-covered bloody body on their front pages.

"Shot Like a Dog" screamed one British headline.

The following day, police arrested Wiggins' girlfriend Patsy Jones after an intensive manhunt to find the actual shooter. In a full confession, Jones admitted that as Wiggins pulled his van next to the Rakebrand's rented Toyota, she stuck a .30-caliber rifle out the window and pulled the trigger. She had been "annoyed" that the tourists were attempting to outrun their "bump and rob." Only four days before the shooting, Jones had been released from a Dade County jail in Ft. Lauderdale on armed robbery charges that had been dropped.

Also arrested and charged with first-degree murder and armed robbery was nineteen-year-old Alvin Charles Hudson, an unemployed laborer from the Bahamas who was a passenger in the van at the time of the crime.

According to police, the trio had been driving around the airport, specifically watching the rental car lots while waiting for the night's final inbound flights to arrive. After the shooting, Wiggins and Jones sped off, only to return to the scene in a stolen car to see what the gunshot had done. It was only after they saw the police and Rakebrand's body underneath a sheet, that they realized they had crossed the line from armed robbers to murderers.

What makes it all the more tragic is that the Rakebrands had been aware of the dangers of vacationing in South Florida. Before they had arrived, seven tourists had been killed in the Sunshine State, including the infamous slaying just six months earlier of German vacationer Barbara Meller-Jensen, a thirty-nine-year-old mother of two sons. Shortly after eight thirty p.m., on April 2, Meller-Jensen had steered her red rental Ford Taurus from the Alamo lot with her children, Alexander, age six and Daria, age two and her seventy-one-year-old mother Annemarie. Less than five miles away, Meller-Jensen, possibly tired from nine hours of traveling, got lost. She navigated her car to N.W. 62nd Street, not knowing this bleak urban terrain of Miami's Liberty City neighborhood was among the most impoverished and crime-ridden areas of the state.

Suddenly, her rental car was rammed from behind. When Meller-Jensen made the mistake of getting out of her car to check the damage, two men emerged from the car that struck hers, beat her, threw her to the ground and took her purse. As they fled, the attackers ran over Barbara Meller-Jensen, killing her as six-year-old Alexander watched in horror.

As it turned out, Meller-Jensen's murder was for nothing. All of her valuables spilled from her purse during the scuffle.

Just a week before Meller-Jensen's murder, Karl Wilhelm Schmidt, age fifty, and his fifteen-year-old son, Kristopher, also German tourists, were shot when four teenagers smashed their rental car window and stole a bag before running off. The bullet went through Karl's leg and lodged in Kristopher's leg. Both survived the attack.

No arrests were ever made in either case.

Knowing all of this, the Rakebrands had planned around the possibility of violence. They had mapped out their rental car route in advance, keeping only to the main roads. They stashed their valuables out of sight and drove briskly.

Only one week later, thirty-four-year-old British taxi driver Gary Colley was shot and killed at a highway rest stop just outside of Tallahassee.

Colley and his girlfriend, Margaret Jagger, both from West Yorkshire, had been halfway through a two-week vacation. They had been on the road for hours before pulling over in their rented Chevy Cavalier to take a nap. Sometime in the early hours of the morning, they were startled awake by a tapping at the driver's side window. Three teens had approached the car, demanding money. Within moments, the shooting started. Colley was hit in the neck and died at the scene.

The insane rash of senseless tourist murders that plagued Florida , otherwise known as the "State of Terror" as it was first dubbed by news outlets around the globe, started on October 6, 1992 with the slaying of Brit Keith Thompson. He and his fiancée, Ann Sole, age thirty-four, had pulled into the parking lot at a forty dollar a night Comfort Inn and were unloading their luggage when two armed men approached and demanded money. When Thompson became initially hesitant, the robbers opened fire and ran away, leaving Sole to hold her boyfriend's head in her lap and try in vain to give him mouth-to-mouth as he died in her arms.

Again, no arrests were ever made in the murders of Gary Colley or Keith Thompson.

Two months after Thompson's killing, German Rudi Rihlott was shot to death in Fort Meyers while enjoying an early evening stroll on December 6. A little more than three weeks later, Canadian airline executive Marc Nadeau was in Lake Worth visiting his elderly father. Nadeau was walking back from a trip to the corner store for milk when he was shot in the head twice and died as his five-year-old son Francis watched in terror.

On January 26, 1993, Canadian Ralph Passero was gunned down in his car during a robbery attempt in Sunny Isles.

In Miami, just four days later, forty-seven-year-old Venezuelan diplomat Jesus Alberto Delgado, was shot and killed during another mugging attempt. Even after the robbers had gotten Delgado's wallet, they shot him in the head just above his right eye. Delgado, out for the evening with friends on their way to attend a dinner being held in his honor, was pronounced dead from severe brain trauma.

No one was ever arrested for the murder.

Less than a month before Meller-Jensen's bump-and-run slaying, German Jorg Schell, fifty-nine, was fatally shot after coming to the aid of his wife, Sonya, during a robbery and car-jacking attempt outside of a motel not far from the Air Force base in Homestead. The killer, sixteen-year-old Damon Peterson, was arrested along with his two buddies, Morrie Bryant and Jonathan Williams.

Born in 1976, Peterson seemed destined for a life of crime after growing up watching his crack-addicted mother do drugs and get beaten by all of her boyfriends. By the age of ten, he was living on the street, eating out of trash cans and scavenging to survive as a regular at unincorporated NW Miami-Dade's Little River Park, a wasteland of homeless, junkies and hookers. At twelve, Peterson was arrested for heaving bricks at vehicles from an overpass. Six months later, he was picked up for breaking into cars. By his thirteenth birthday, Peterson was again arrested for car burglary and grand theft auto. After a short stint in juvie, Peterson was again arrested for smashing a car window with a spark plug and stealing a purse.

According to Sonya Schell, the telltale rental car license plate was why she and her husband were spotted as tourists and targeted by the robbers after leaving a nearby restaurant.

In February of 1993, Florida Governor Lawton Chiles issued an emergency executive order for rental car companies to abandon the Y-and-Z designated license plates.

By the time of Barbara Meller-Jensen's senseless murder on April 2, some six weeks later, a stunning ninety-four percent of Florida rental cars still carried the troublesome tags. It was only in 1994, after a dozen foreign tourists had been murdered in Florida that the state finally abolished the Y and Z license plates. Instead, the new state law required that all leased vehicles in the state (of which rental cars make up ninety percent) bear a special sticker, more or less defeating the purpose of this somewhat questionable security measure.

Though the early 1990s had been indelibly marred by this rash of tourist slayings, it is well up to debate whether Florida remains safe for tourists even today.

In early August 2006, twenty-two-year-old Brandon Antron Rolle, a convicted felon who had done three separate stints in prison and had just been released less than a month before, strolled into a Miami-area police station stating he had, "Something to clear up." It was during questioning by detectives that Rolle admitted to being the man police had been searching for in the shooting death of a fifty-four-year-old man visiting from Chicago.

Ronald Gentile had come to Miami to celebrate his son's seventeenth birthday. On July 29, 2006, Gentile and his son Paul spent the day together sightseeing and then shopping at the Nike store at South Miami's Sunset Place Mall, the same mall where Paul worked nights at a restaurant.

After dropping Paul off, Gentile got into his rental car, a Chevrolet Cobalt and got onto Southwest 57th Avenue to head back to his ex-wife's house in Kendall for dinner. Unfamiliar with the area, Gentile got lost. By mistake, he turned right on U.S. 1 and headed north, finally ending up in Coconut Grove.

Sometime around five thirty, Gentile stopped his rental car at the intersection of Washington Avenue and Jefferson Street. There, he rolled down his window to ask a stranger for directions.

To Gentile's misfortune, that stranger happened to be recently released felon, Brandon Rolle. Instead of helping Gentile, Rolle reached in and snatched a chain from around Gentile's wrist and fired one shot into the car with a .380 Bersa. Witnesses heard the shot and saw the fatally wounded Gentile stagger from the vehicle before collapsing onto the ground.

Along with Rolle's admission, police also found Rolle's fingerprints on the driver's side door of Gentile's rented Cobalt. A Miami convenience store clerk also testified that Rolle had attempted to use Gentile's stolen credit card and had even been so bold as to try and sell him Gentile's cell phone.

Rolle's girlfriend even dimed him, telling detectives that Rolle had begged her to concoct an alibi. She showed them a photo of Rolle taken at a nightclub, wearing Gentile's bracelet, his hand and fingers extended outward as if to pantomime holding a gun.

On September 17, 2010, over four years after the crime, Brandon Antron Rolle, a lifetime criminal who suffered a tragic upbringing and in the end chose to take the life of a stranger in a robbery gone bad, went on trial for first degree murder. In early February of the following year, after delivering a verdict of guilty, a jury recommended Brandon Rolle be put to death in Florida's electric chair.

Much to the outrage of many in the community and the family of the victims, Judge Dennis Murphy chose to override the death sentence and instead remanded Brandon Antron Rolle to prison for the rest of his life without the possibility of parole.

But it's not always the presence of a rental car that precipitates fatal violence against Florida tourists.

April 15, 2011. It was a Friday night out for Brits James Kouzaris, twenty-four and James Cooper, twenty-five, who were on a holiday to the Sunshine State. To commemorate his past travels, Kouzaris had proudly plastered his Facebook page with photos taken in places like Ecuador, Taiwan, Argentina, Vietnam and Laos. Along with university friend Cooper and Cooper's family, Kouzaris had been staying in Longboat Key, a tony area along Florida's central west coast better known for its condo communities and tennis courts. However, for nightlife, the pair travelled a dozen miles into Sarasota. Late Friday night turned into early Saturday morning as Kouzaris and Cooper hung out at Smokin' Joes, a sports bar on Main Street and a music hotspot nearby known as The Gator Club.

Then sometime around three a.m., about an hour after the bars had closed, Kouzaris and Cooper were found dead in the middle of Carver Court, a one-way road in a housing project in the impoverished neighborhood of Newtown just about a couple miles from Sarasota's Main Street. Both had been shot multiple times, their dead bodies surrounded by bullet casings.

Within three days, police had apprehended sixteen-year-old Shawn Tyson for the murder of Kouzaris and Cooper, a charge Tyson denied despite being discovered in possession of the same caliber bullets used in their killing. However, according to a three hundred-page document released by the state's attorney's office, Tyson confessed to a fellow inmate only twenty-four hours after the shooting, saying, "Yeah, I did it."

After being asked by the inmate what had happened, Tyson reportedly replied, "It's trill," a local slang word meaning, "gangster."

Shortly afterwards, a taxi driver came forth and reported he had taken Kouzaris and Cooper to a 7-Eleven in Newtown. Both, he reported, were extremely drunk.

The same jailhouse witness who reported Tyson's confession to authorities later recalled Tyson's account of the crime. Tyson had seen two strangers staggering drunk down the road. He approached them from behind and opened fire.

Though it may never be known what led Kouzaris and Cooper to a one-way street in a housing project thousands of miles away from their suburban British homes, some have speculated that perhaps the pair were out looking for drugs or sex. Maybe they were just lost and took a wrong turn that proved to be their last.

If it weren't enough to be afraid of Florida's violent criminal element, it also seems that danger for tourists comes in the unlikely form of the police as well. Twenty-nine-year-old Husien Shehada, a Woodbridge, Virginia limo driver was fatally shot by police on a palm tree-lined street two blocks from the ocean in Miami Beach at four thirty a.m. as he walked with his brother, Samer.

Shehada's story is a tragic tale tinged with tones of stupidity, domestic violence and possible racism. Husein and Samer Shehada, both Palestinain-Americans, traveled to Miami from Virginia along with their girlfriends with one plan: party. After a dispute outside a nightclub on Washington Avenue around one a.m., Samer got into a vicious fight with his girlfriend and threw her to the ground. A pair of men witnessing Samer hitting his girlfriend stepped in to intervene and in doing so, roughed him up. According to the police report, Samer and his girlfriend returned to their room at the Lowes Miami Beach hotel.

Husein, who had been out partying at another club with his girlfriend, later returned to the hotel. Upon hearing of the evening's events, it was Husein's suggestion that they go looking for the two men who had beaten up Samer. In an attempt to appear armed, Samer clenched a wooden coat hanger under his shirt while Husein wielded a green glass beer bottle under his.

It was the bouncer at Twist, the club Samer had been earlier thrown out from, who recognized him and thought he had come back with a gun looking to retaliate. At first glance, the bouncer mistook the coat hanger for the folded stock of a rifle. He dialed 911, as coincidentally did several other passers-by who also thought the pair were armed.

According to one source, it was reported the two brothers, "looked menacing."

Screeching up in front of Twist were two police cars. Officers, guns drawn, began barking commands to Husein and Samer. When Husein allegedly failed to respond, a patrolman opened fire, believing that Husein was reaching for a gun.

Husein Shehada died later at Jackson Memorial Hospital. During questioning, both Samer and Husein's girlfriends were asked several times by investigators if they spoke Arabic.

Within seventy-two hours, Adam Tavss, the officer who fired the fatal shot, was allowed to return to active duty. During his first shift back in uniform, Tavss was involved in a second shooting death, this time while responding to a report of a carjacking in progress.

It bears mentioning that although Tavss was eventually (and controversially) cleared of any wrongdoing in the death of Husein Shehada, he was arrested on May 24, 2010 after Miami-Dade police found a fully-operational marijuana grow lab in his home. He has since been removed from the police force and was sentenced to two years house arrest.

The stories of Florida tourist violence are numerous. The crimes so senseless, one would think that underneath those sun-bleached skies walk countless predators just looking for an unsuspecting target to unleash their evil upon. For what could be the most nightmarish scenario of all, one can look no further than the tragic story of fifteen-year-old Courtney Wilkes.

A smart girl with a pretty smile and what seemed to be a bright future, Courtney Wilkes was a straight-A honor student from Toombs County, Georgia. With her two younger siblings and her parents, she had come to Seagrove Beach, a sleepy resort town on the Florida Panhandle named for the thick groves of windswept oak trees that line the shore. She was shy. She had never been on a date before. It was there on June 16, 2011 that she met a twenty-one-year-old guy with a pleasant smile and dark brown eyes. Together they went for a walk.

Three hours had passed and Courtney's mother grew worried. At six minutes past four p.m., she called the sheriff's office. During their search, Courtney's father spotted the boy she had been walking with. Sheriffs took Steven Cozzie into custody without incident.

Shortly afterwards they found Courtney's body in a wooded area nearby where she had been beaten, strangled and sexually assaulted.

It was during a press conference the following day that Sheriff Mike Adkinson almost cried as he recalled the horrifying details of what he described as an "extremely violent encounter." Adkinson made it very clear to all in attendance what he thought of Cozzie, a homeless drifter who had been kicked out of his parents' home about a week earlier. "This is a situation where you had one individual who obviously has evil in his heart. If he has a soul, it's absent."

Cozzie, who had been living on the streets, showed no remorse for what he had done. If you didn't know the circumstances behind his booking photo, you could easily mistake Cozzie's wry smile for a high school yearbook picture instead of the gleam of an alleged psychopath.

What is it about Florida that makes it such a magnet for tourist violence?

According to former Tampa area police officer P.W. Fenton, it's a combination of the anonymity of tourist centers, the idea that the majority of the population is "just visiting" and the helpless nature of a tourist not knowing their way around. Most criminals are well aware that visitors generally have no friends, neighbors or co-workers expecting to hear from them at a certain time or place. Also, given the slow grind of the wheels of our criminal justice system, it is rare that a robbery victim will return from overseas to testify against a perp.

It is also impossible to ignore the factors of poverty. According to U.S. Census figures, more than one in six Floridians live below the poverty line.

Prompted by a rash of armed robberies not far from Disneyland in the heart of Orlando's tourist district, Orange County Sheriff Jerry Demings launched T.O.P.S., the Tourist Oriented Policing Squad in March 2010.

In 2011, the F.B.I. released a report indicating that Orlando is the third most dangerous city in the U.S.

CARIBBEAN DREAMS GONE BAD

"Come back to Jamaica…and make it your home," cooed the deep voice, lulling travelers into considering a trip to the island getaway as their televisions played back the type of tropical postcard-perfect imagery that Jamaica conjures up in the mind. This was the tagline for a long-running series of advertisements, mostly visible in TV commercials strategically set to run in American homes during the coldest months of winter. How could you not want to sit by the beach, eating deep-fried conch and sipping a rum-filled beverage from a coconut shell as steel drums pinged out lively rump-shaking tunes?

It's an intoxicating thought to say the least—the type of memories that last a lifetime.

As would having someone try to hijack your plane back home—which is exactly what happened to CanJet flight 918 in Montego Bay on April 20, 2009 as a twenty-year old man forced his way though Sangster International Airport security and boarded the plane, gun in hand. At ten p.m., forty minutes before the flight was set to take off for Halifax, Nova Scotia, Stephen Fray rushed past the last people to board and brandished a pistol to the shock of the flight's six crew and one hundred seventy-four passengers. He then fired a warning shot and demanded to be taken to Cuba.

During the next thirty minutes, Fray waved his gun around, pointing it directly at several people, including a group of extremely terrified deaf travelers who were limited in the amount of communication they received. For many passengers, the comparison to 9/11, and the heartstopping fear that this madman could be willing to crash the jet as part of some crusade was unavoidable.

Police cordoned off the airport and surrounded the plane. A quick-thinking flight attendant decided to make a bold move. She convinced the passengers that they should attempt to bribe their hijacker. Fray accepted the deal and allowed the passengers and two of the crew to get off the plane in exchange for their valuables, purses, passports and wallets. The rest of the crew would have to stay onboard. As heavily-armed soldiers arrived on the scene, things grew tense. Fray's father was located and brought in to help negotiate Stephen off the plane. "My son is mentally challenged," he pleaded with authorities. As hours passed, even the Prime Minister of Jamaica, Bruce Golding, attempted to negotiate with Stephen Fray.

But as dawn broke, negotiations for the release of the remaining hostages broke down and Golding ordered the police to take back the plane by force. At six forty a.m., two members of the Jamaica Defence Force Counter Terrorism Operations Group disguised in CanJet flight crew uniforms covertly entered through the cockpit window. One of the operatives, impersonating the co-pilot, overpowered Stephen Fray, ending the eight-hour ordeal.

And in the swift turn of the wheels of Canadian justice, on May 1, 2009, Stephen Fray was charged with assault, robbery with aggravation, illegal possession of a firearm and ammunition, shooting with intent to harm, and breaching the Civil Aviation Act along with, of course, attempted hijacking. He was convicted and sentenced to twenty years behind bars.

It was later alleged that Fray had been distraught over a breakup.

Fortunately, nobody was hurt in this particular isolated incident. However, it does underscore that many of the Caribbean Islands are far from being as carefree and safe as one may want to believe. And though Jamaica suffers from high levels of poverty, drug trafficking and a jaw-dropping homicide rate, the U.S. Department of State alleges that violent crimes in Jamaica rarely involve foreign victims.

But rare doesn't mean *never*. On August 11, 2006, twenty-seven-year old Australian tourist Brian Johnston was found in a puddle of his own blood, beaten and stabbed to death in his ransacked room at the Gloucestershire Hotel. Far from being the wrong side of the tracks, Brian's brutal murder happened in the popular "Hip Strip" district of Montego Bay, renowned for its restaurants, bars and many area hotspots to relax and play. According to reports in the local newspaper, *Jamaica Gleaner*, Johnston was discovered stabbed in the head, chest and neck and had a large wound over one eye. Evidence showed Brian had struggled with an assailant because some items in his hotel room, including a bedside lamp and a vase, had been smashed and a large dirty footprint not belonging to the victim was found on the bed.

Within days a prostitute was arrested. The motive, allegedly, was robbery.

Brian Johnston was in fact the second foreigner to be killed in the area in less than a month. On July 20, a pregnant thirty-seven-year old Swedish woman was found mutilated in Hanover parish. No arrest was ever made in that case.

In 2010, the U.S. Department of State renewed its travel advisory for Jamaica, claiming that *a possibility exists for violence and/or civil unrest in the greater Kingston metropolitan area. There are unconfirmed reports of criminal gang members amassing in the Kingston area, as well as mobilization of Jamaican defense forces.* Also adding that, *If the situation ignites, there is a possibility of severe disruptions of movement within Kingston, including blocking of access roads to the Norman Manley International Airport. The possibility exists that unrest could spread beyond the general Kingston area. U.S. Embassy Kingston is taking extra security precautions.*

How dangerous is Jamaica? According to recent crime statistics, this island nation covering four thousand two hundred forty-three square miles and home to two point seven million people sees approximately fifty-two homicides per one hundred thousand people. In comparison, New York City is home to less than seven homicides per one hundred thousand. Currently, Jamaica is jockeying for the world murder capital crown with current title-holders Columbia and South Africa.

And as a side note, it should be very clearly expressed that gay travelers to Jamaica run a very high risk of violence. Homosexuality is illegal in this island nation where many still point to the brutal abduction and murder of Jamaican gay-rights and AIDS activist, Steve Harvey, along with anti-gay lyrics to popular Dancehall music hits as a chilling indicator where attitudes still lay.

But it is not only violence that forms the only danger to those visiting the wonderful and sandy shores of the Caribbean. Though nobody ever wants to think about it—or just would prefer to be in denial—along with visiting any tropical paradise full of activities comes the risk of possible injury and death.

On June 4, 2011, Victor and Crystal Rodriguez were married in Roseville, California. Both were such lovers of the outdoors and sports that Crystal's bridesmaids were dressed in black and teal, the color of their favorite team, the San Jose Sharks. The pair spent a few days at Disneyland before heading to the sunny beaches of the Bahamas. Everyone they knew thought the attractive twenty-two-year old newlyweds had their entire lives ahead of them. Instead, a sudden tragedy ended their love far too soon.

It was the last day of a dream honeymoon in the Bahamas. Shortly after one p.m. on June 16, Crystal and Victor were parasailing on Lucayan Beach when the harness holding them to the ride's parachute suddenly snapped, sending the newlyweds plummeting and tumbling into the ocean. Though water can make for a safe landing from a few feet above, Victor and Crystal fell from more than two hundred feet, striking the ocean's surface with deadly force. As hundreds of beach-goers watched in horror, Victor's lung was punctured and several of his bones were broken.

Crystal was killed instantly.

For parasail ride operator Ocean Motion, Crystal Rodriguez's death was the second tragedy to befall them in less than two weeks. On June 3, Keith Rollings, a seventeen-year old employee of the company was riding a jet ski to William's Town Beach when he disappeared. Though the jet ski was recovered miles away, Rollings was nowhere to be found. Days later, his body was discovered floating face down in shallow water.

Sadly, it's not just the ocean that poses a severe drowning risk. On December 28, 2010, while enjoying the Jacuzzi at the Sandals Royal Bahamian Resort, thirty-three-year old John Van Hoy Jr. dunked his body below the surface of the churning water only to be trapped by the extremely strong suction of the hot tub's outlet drain. Van Hoy Jr., a man in excellent shape, capable of bench-pressing over three hundred pounds, could not free himself from the force sucking him to the bottom. It was only when his fiancée, Nicole Cleaveland noticed he hadn't resurfaced that she realized something was wrong. Screaming for help, she jumped fully clothed into the Jacuzzi trying to free John Van Hoy Jr. from the power of the drain's suction. According to eyewitness accounts, she called out to a Royal Bahamian Resort employee who ignored her pleas for help and actually walked away.

There was no shut-off switch nearby. No way to stop the pump.

After hearing Nicole's screams, several resort guests attempted to come to John Van Hoy Jr's rescue, trying to pull him free. Collectively they pulled in vain until one man braced his legs against the Jacuzzi wall as others yanked on Van Hoy Jr's limbs until they were able to get him out of the suction's deadly grip. Tragically, John Van Hoy Jr. was declared dead at the hospital.

According to a lawsuit filed by the estate of John Van Hoy Jr. against Sandals, at no point during the entire rescue did a single resort employee attempt to turn off the Jacuzzi's pump, nor did any resort employee seem able or even willing to attempt CPR on John Van Hoy Jr. during the forty-five minutes before the ambulance arrived. It is unimaginable to even think of the excruciating terror and pain suffered by John Van Hoy Jr. in those final moments of his life.

Also quite disturbing is the following claim found inside the complaint:

After Hoy's death, Sandals' employees tried to remove the phone from Cleaveland's room "to prevent contact with friends, family and local assistance," the family claims. The Jamaica-based hotel chain and its Delaware-based marketing representative, Unique Vacations, then "subjected Nicole Cleaveland to interrogation in which they attempted to suggest that John Van Hoy, Jr., or she were somehow at fault for the death."

One always tends to believe that they are safe within the boundaries of any resort. The terrible truth is that tragedy can strike anywhere and anyone. Even more frightening is the idea that those in need of help didn't have to die.

In April of 2011, five-year old Brooklyn Rattai was pulled unconscious from the Aquaventure water park pool at the Atlantis Resort on Paradise Island. According to eyewitness Toni Randall, a certified nurse from Michigan, she came to Brooklyn's aid immediately when she saw the child wasn't breathing. Another guest, an emergency room doctor, performed a jaw thrust to open Brooklyn's airway. However, when lifeguards arrived at the scene, they ordered Randall and the doctor back. Randall, who had been trained in cardiac life support and had documentation in her hotel room to prove it, advised the inexperienced teenage lifeguards not to perform CPR on the child because Brooklyn still had a pulse.

Instead, the teenage lifeguards ignored the two medical professionals and, according to Randall, incorrectly administered CPR on Brooklyn, not even knowing to check her pulse or turning the drowned girl over to prevent water from going into her lungs.

They told nurse Randall her documents weren't valid in the Bahamas. She was ordered to stay back or else they were going to call the police.

Three days later, Brooklyn Rattai died in a Bahamian hospital, though there has been great speculation whether or not it was the actions of the lifeguards that ultimately resulted in her death.

Eleven years earlier, Atlantis was also the site of the drowning death of twelve-year old Chad Humphreys who was sucked headfirst into a fourteen-inch wide pool drainpipe and killed while snorkeling at the resort's Paradise Lagoon. The force of the suction was so massive that Chad's right ear was torn from his head and his entire five-foot-one-inch long body, save for his feet and swim fins, were trapped inside the pipe.

Then in 2002, yet another tragedy struck the resort. Two-year-old Paul Gallagher was on the Atlantis beach when an unmanned boat broke free and ran up onto the sand, striking and killing the toddler. The cause of death was listed as blunt force trauma to the head, causing a fractured skull and hemorrhaging of the brain. Later, Paul's death was ruled "accidental" by a Bahamian Coroner's court jury, though it has been alleged by tourism website bahamasb2b.com that, "crooked lawyers and politicians in the Bahamas made sure the family got nowhere in the dysfunctional and corrupt Bahamian courts."

Sadly, it is often these allegations of corruption that seem to further taint the image of the

Bahamas. In 2009, after actor John Travolta's son, Jett, died following a seizure in which he violently struck his head on the bathtub of the family's vacation home, an ambulance driver and a Bahamian senator conspired to blackmail the Travoltas. The plan was to extort millions by threatening to release a photo to the U.S. tabloids of Jett as he lay dying unless the Travoltas coughed up twenty-five million dollars. In the end, the case was brought to court, ending in a mistrial. A second attempt to prosecute the alleged extortionists was later dropped at the request of the Travolta family who no longer could bear the great emotional pain the continuing litigation brought them in the wake of the loss of their only teenage son.

THE NATALEE HOLLOWAY DISAPPEARANCE: EVERY PARENT'S NIGHTMARE

The kids had been away. It had been a long weekend of relaxing at their lake house in Hot Springs, Arkansas. Beth Twitty was headed home to welcome her daughter back from the class trip of a lifetime when the phone rang.

It was the type of call that lives on the darkest edge of every parent's worst nightmare.

Natalee Holloway had not come back to her room the night before. Nobody knew her whereabouts. Right away, her mother knew something was terribly wrong. Natalee was not the kind of girl to be late for anything.

So what exactly happened? How did this pretty blonde girl disappear without a trace?

On January 12, 2012, almost seven years after she vanished from Aruba, Natalee Holloway was declared dead in an Alabama court of law. To this day, whatever happened to Natalee Ann Holloway remains a mystery that may never be solved.

For a cold case with so few clues, what remains are the definite facts. She had left the country on an unofficial graduation trip. Natalee, a member of the National Honor Society, had earned a full scholarship to the University of Alabama where she planned to pursue pre-med in the fall. The five day blast to Aruba with one hundred twenty-four of her classmates from Mountain Brook High School in the wealthy suburb of Birmingham, Alabama was the final hurrah of their time together —a wild non-stop bacchanal in a Caribbean paradise that none would ever forget.

For underage party-goers, Aruba makes for an ideal getaway. Here on this flat, riverless island world-famous for white sand beaches and festive atmosphere, the legal drinking age is eighteen and even that is not very strictly enforced. Tourists arrive looking to relax, let loose and have a good time, and Natalee's school trip was no different than countless others that had come before. According to Holloway's classmates, alcohol intake by the chaperoned group was excessive. Natalee drank all day every day, starting each morning with cocktails. On two separate mornings, she was so hung-over that she didn't show up for breakfast. It was par for the course. The kids on the trip were a rowdy bunch, making noise at all hours and switching rooms. Management at The Holiday Inn where they were staying made it clear the group from Mountain Brook wouldn't be welcome back the following year.

On Monday, May 30, the night before her class was set to return home to Alabama, Holloway went to party with some classmates over at Carlos 'n Charlies, a popular Aruban bar and night club. It was here Natalee bumped into a charming seventeen-year-old Dutch kid named Joran van der Sloot who lived on Aruba and attended the Aruba International School, where he, too, was a member of the honors program. Sometime around one a.m., in the wee hours of her last night on the island, Natalee surprised her friends by leaving the club with Joran, an ordinary boy that Mountain Brook classmate Ruth McVay later claimed Natalee first met at a blackjack table in their hotel's casino the night before. In fact, according to McVay that night, Joran van der Sloot wasn't even flirting. It was Natalee who introduced herself to him before walking off.

Monday nights, bars close early on Aruba. Perhaps it was the mob of people waiting for taxis that made Natalee accept a ride from Joran. After reassuring her friends she was "okay," Natalee got into a car with two of Joran's friends, brothers Deepak, twenty-one, and Satish Kalpoe, eighteen. At the next intersection, Deepak Kalpoe stopped his car. Some of Natalee's classmates waiting for taxis implored her to get out and come with them. She refused, saying she wanted to go for a drive with her three new friends.

By ten thirty the next morning, Natalee didn't appear for her return flight. Back inside her room at the Holiday Inn her packed luggage and passport were found just where she had left them.

Immediately, Aruban authorities initiated a search across the island. Natalee's distraught mother, Beth, along with stepfather, George, a successful businessman better known to friends as "Jug," arrived by plane hours later along with family friends.

Sometime between three and five a.m. the following morning, on Tuesday, May 31, 2005, Natalee's mother and several of her friends confronted Deepak Kalpoe and Joran van der Sloot outside of the van der Sloot family home. It was here that van der Sloot made his first admission, that sometime around two a.m. the previous night they dropped Natalee off in front of her hotel. According to a local D.J., Charles Croes, who was there at the confrontation, van der Sloot appeared scared and claimed Natalee had been doing drugs and possibly drinking. Over and over van der Sloot offered to help in any way.

In the first days, hundreds of local volunteers joined the search for Natalee. Even the Aruban government, possibly sensing the public relations nightmare Natalee's disappearance was causing in the global media, gave thousands of civil servants the day off to participate in the search for the missing American girl. Overwhelmed, the Arubans appealed to U.S. Secretary of State Condoleeza Rice for help. Since Aruba is part of the Kingdom of the Netherlands, fifty Dutch Marines were sent to conduct an extensive search of the shoreline and surrounding water.

No sign of Natalee was found. The best leads investigators had in the case were the three young men who had allegedly been the last ones seen with her. On the third day after the disappearance, Aruban police put the Kalpoe brothers and Joran van der Sloot under surveillance, observing their movements, tapping their phones and monitoring their email.

Still, the trio proclaimed their innocence. Voluntarily, the three boys gave statements at the police station. Joran van der Sloot and Deepak Kalpoe repeated what they had told the angry group in front of van der Sloot's house. Deepak's brother Satish, who had not been present at the confrontation, made the same statement as Deepak and van der Sloot: after driving around to the lighthouse and then Marriott Beach, they dropped Natalee off at the Holiday Inn around two a.m., where she stumbled in the parking lot but refused help from van der Sloot. They told police that before driving off, they witnessed Natalee being approached by a man in a security guard uniform.

On June 5, two arrests were made. On suspicion of murder and kidnapping, police picked up Nick John and Abraham Jones, former security guards from the nearby Allegro Hotel. According to locals, the pair had a reputation for cruising hotels along the beach, trying to pick up women. One had even been in trouble with the law before.

Four days later, on June 9, after being placed under extreme pressure by the Holloway family and the worldwide press the case had received, police brought van der Sloot and the Kalpoes into custody—a move that may have ultimately compromised the investigation by forcing Aruban officials to make legal moves on a case they had yet to accumulate enough evidence to solve.

The Kalpoes and van der Sloot continued to profess their innocence. But now, separated from one another, their stories began to change. According to the Kalpoe brothers, they dropped van der Sloot and Natalee off at Mariott Beach around one forty or one forty-five a.m. and then drove home where Satish claimed he went right to sleep. However, Deepak told police he got on his computer around two a.m., offering login information as supposed proof. Then at two forty a.m., he said he received a cell phone call from van der Sloot asking for a ride from Mariott Beach. At three a.m., van der Sloot allegedly called again to say he left Natalee on the beach and was walking home alone.

On June 13, security guards Nick John and Abraham Jones were released from custody and charges against them were dismissed. Still, doubts lingered about Joran van der Sloot's story. One version corroborated Deepak's accounting about being dropped at Marriott Beach with Natalee. Except, according to van der Sloot, Deepak Kalpoe did pick him up, alone, and took him home. Cell phone signal triangulation based upon calls made by van der Sloot first place him at Marriott Beach at two forty a.m, and then back home sometime around three fifteen a.m. That version then changed to claim he again walked home.

However, indisputable facts make whatever truth may lay in these statements a whole lot muddier.

Deepak's computer login record showed that he initiated online activity at two a.m. He claims he logged off an hour later. However, van der Sloot's computer records indicate Deepak sent him an instant message at three twenty-five. Sometime between three forty-six and four thirty a.m, van der Sloot visited porn sites backseatbangers.com and nastydollars.com where he downloaded two movies.

At one point, van der Sloot even went so far as to suggest to his interrogators that after dropping him off at his house, Deepak went back to the beach where he raped and murdered Natalee. When confronted with his computer records, van der Sloot retracted the accusation. Once more, his story changed to say that it was actually Deepak's brother Satish who had picked him up and driven him home. Natalee wanted to be left on the beach. She had asked him to stay with her, but van der Sloot told her he had to get up early to go to school the next day.

During this time, the investigation began to spiral out of control. Accusations were running like a rampant wildfire. On June 22, Joran's father, Paulus van der Sloot, a renowned local judge himself, was detained for questioning and then later arrested that day only to be released days later. On Monday, July 4, the same day the Royal Netherlands Air Force deployed three F-16 fighter jets equipped with infrared scanners to search the coast, the Kalpoe brothers were released from jail.

However, because Aruban law allows detainment of a suspect for months without charging them with a crime, Joran van der Sloot would spend another sixty days behind bars facing intense interrogation, including sleep deprivation and questioning late into the night. During this time van der Sloot never cracked. In none of the versions of his story did he admit to causing any harm to Natalee or knowing what happened to her. Though the details of van der Sloot's stories changed, including recollection of geographical fixtures at the beach where he had allegedly left Natalee, one thing remained constant: the maintaining of his innocence.

During this time a local gardener came forward with a startling admission; sometime between two thirty and three a.m, the morning of Natalee's disappearance, he had allegedly seen Joran van der Sloot and the two Kalpoe brothers driving into the Aruba Racquet Club not far from Marriott Beach. On the strength of this claim, a small pond on the edge of the premises was drained. Though some had initially cited this as a massive breakthrough in the case, unfortunately no evidence was found. Shortly thereafter, another tip, one that claimed an eyewitness had seen men burying a blonde-haired woman in a landfill, initiated another focused search. Cadaver dogs were brought in, again to no avail. Then on July 18, a park ranger walking along the beach discovered a piece of duct tape that had strands of blonde hair attached to it. The clue was immediately sent to the FBI's crime lab in Quantico, Virginia to be tested against a sample of Natalee's DNA, but it was quickly determined the hair belonged to someone else.

A week later the reward for Natalee's safe return was increased to one million U.S. dollars.

By this time, the Twitty family's non-stop hounding of the Aruban authorities and Beth Twitty's near-daily appearances on television was bringing added pressure to a case that had, so far, produced very little in the way of credible leads. In an attempt to pressure the Kalpoe brothers, police arrested Deepak and Satish along with friend, twenty-one-year-old Freddy Arambatzis on August 26. Arambatzis was an attractive suspect due to previous suspicion that he, along with van der Sloot and the Kalpoes, had taken photographs and had physical contact with an underage girl at some point before Natalee's disappearance. Despite more interrogations and protests by Aruban prosecutors looking to continue to try and build a case against the only suspects they had so far, an Aruban judge released Joran van der Sloot, Arambatzis and the Kalpoe brothers from jail. To complicate the investigation even further, no restrictions were placed upon the four suspects, allowing them to leave Aruba if they so desired.

Regardless of the extremely frustrating way Dutch law allowed the last three people known to have seen Holloway alive to walk, Beth Twitty refused to give up and the world media was eager to enable her outrage. Publicly, she pointed fingers at the Aruban police. The fact that Joran's father, Paulus, was an influential judge did not escape criticism. The implications of possible cover-ups were hard to avoid, as the world watched this case slip through the fingers of the law. Repeatedly, Beth

Twitty called for tourists to boycott the island of Aruba until there was justice for Natalee.

The Kalpoe brothers did everything in their power to disappear from plain sight. Curiously though, Joran van der Sloot decided to take it upon himself to fight the Twitty's media barrage by appearing in several televised interviews to tell his side of the story. The problem was his side kept changing. During widely-hyped TV interviews for ABC's investigative news magazine, "Primetime" and then again in a March 2006 Fox News interview aired over three nights, van der Sloot claimed he planned to have consensual sex with Natalie after they left Carlos 'n Charlies. He said they had planned to go to his house. "I asked her if she wanted to have sex, and she was fine with it," he told ABC's Chris Cuomo. However, things didn't go as planned. Instead of van der Sloot's house, they ended up at the beach. Natalie, he claims, still wanted to have sex, but he didn't have a condom and didn't want to do it with a stranger without protection.

His regret was allegedly leaving Holloway at the beach alone, though he admitted that in Aruba, he did have a reputation of being a ladies' man, picking up female tourists, having a good time with them and saying goodbye. He told Fox's Greta Van Susteren that he been untruthful about this one small detail because he was certain Natalee would turn up safely.

When questioned about all the lies he had told police, van der Sloot sheepishly admitted he'd have a hard time believing himself either.

Shortly before Aruban Deputy Chief Gerold Dompig left the case, he floated a new twist, one that supposes van der Sloot and the Kalpoe brothers did not murder Natalee Holloway. In Dompig's suggested scenario, Natalee was not driven to the beach, but instead taken to the van der Sloot's home where she died suddenly from an overdose of intoxicants. Though there have been varying accounts of drugs being present during the Mountain Brook trip and contradictory statements as to whether Natalee had ever been seen with narcotics in Aruba, there had always been the possibility the vast amounts of alcohol she had been drinking along with some type of drug van der Sloot and/or the Kalpoes had given her caused her body to go into shock. If this was the case, surmised Dompig, the only crime actually committed by Joran van der Sloot and the Kalpoe brothers was the illegal disposal of Natalee's body.

It was also around this time that Dompig allegedly made a very startling off-the-record statement to Jossy Mansur, editor of Aruba's "Dario" newspaper. According to sources, Dompig claimed that van der Sloot and the Kalpoes admitted having sex with Natalee as she was fading in and out of consciousness.

If this indeed was true, and this admission was indeed made by the suspects, then why weren't they at least charged with rape, an offense that would have brought at least an eight-year prison term?

During an interview with CBS News' Troy Roberts, Dompig claimed that the investigation into Holloway's disappearance had cost more than three million dollars, approximately forty percent of the annual Aruban police budget. Resources had been stretched thin under the extreme scrutiny placed upon it. Mistakes had been made.

It was obvious the case had grown ice cold. Two more arrests of men suspected either of having dealt drugs to Natalee or possibly abducting her were made separately, about a month apart. None of the charges stuck, and both suspects were released within days of being taken into custody. By now almost a year and a half had passed since Natalee vanished. Desperate, the Aruban authorities turned over everything they had to the Dutch National Police.

By April of 2007, Joran van der Sloot had published a book called "The Case of Natalee Holloway" where he continued to maintain his innocence. Unmoved, the Dutch authorities launched a new search of the van der Sloot family residence in Aruba. A diary and a computer were seized. Both were later returned.

Two weeks later, the Kalpoe's home was searched again. Nothing was removed from the house, but in November of that year Satish and Deepak Kalpoe along with Joran van der Sloot were all re-arrested on suspicion of manslaughter based upon what investigators cited as "newly discovered evidence." Because he had left Aruba due to the constant scrutiny, van der Sloot was detained in the Netherlands while the Kalpoes were jailed back in Aruba. However, the "evidence" used to arrest the trio turned out to be yet another desperate smokescreen to see if the boys would finally crack under pressure. A snippet of a chat room conversation by Deepak Kalpoe referring to Natalee Holloway having drowned had been misinterpreted from Papiamento—a Creole dialect spoken on Aruba—to Dutch, when in fact he had only been discussing the tragic story of a teacher who had recently drowned.

In December of 2007, prosecutor Hans Mos had no choice but to watch his only suspects walk away once again. With no other options, he declared the case closed. Ronald Wix, attorney for the Kalpoe brothers told reporters that unless Mos "finds a body in the bathroom of one of these kids, there's no way in hell they can arrest them anymore."

Nearly two years of searching had brought nothing but dead ends. Natalee's stepfather, Jug Twitty who had recently divorced Natalee's mother, said he believed there were people in Aruba who knew what had happened to Natalee, but were not coming forward. He described the decision to let the boys walk for good as, "a sad day for the Aruban people because the officials there are inept."

It would be around this time that circumstances in the Natalee Holloway case began to take a decidedly darker and sinister tone.

A Dutch journalist named Peter R. de Vries came forth on January 31, 2008 to declare he had broken the case. de Vries, a crime reporter and host of one of Netherland's most-watched TV programs, had set up a hidden-camera sting where he claimed Joran van der Sloot had admitted his guilt in the death of Natalee Holloway. "She'll never be found," van der Sloot told Patrick van der Erm, a Dutch businessman and ex-convict who had been used by de Vries to gain Joran's confidence. Sitting in van der Erm's hidden-camera rigged Range Rover, van der Sloot could be seen smoking marijuana and telling how Natalee had gone into convulsions on the beach while they were having sex. According to this new version of the story, van der Sloot panicked. "Suddenly she started shaking and then she didn't say anything," he told his new friend. He explained how he used a nearby pay phone to call a friend for help. When the friend arrived, he and van der Sloot put Natalee's body on a boat, took it out to sea and pushed it into the water.

He said he had tried to revive her. Coldly, he told van der Erm that though she looked dead, he wasn't quite certain she wasn't alive when they dumped her body. At several points, van der Sloot bragged about the financial compensation he was in the process of claiming for his "wrongful accusal."

"I've not lost sleep over this," he added as seven million Dutch people, half the country's population, watched. "The ocean is big."

The day after the interviews aired on Dutch TV, the case was re-opened. An arrest warrant for Joran van der Sloot was requested by the prosecutor; however a Dutch judge denied it, saying that, according to Dutch laws, the televised confessions were not enough to arrest him. Perhaps feeling the same kind of public pressure placed on the Aruban authorities, the prosecutor attempted to appeal the denial. Based upon their ruling that van der Sloot's confession to a camera was still insufficient evidence and that it was inconsistent with the meager evidence in the case, again the request to arrest van der Sloot for Natalee's murder was denied.

During this time, investigators were able to locate "Daury," the "friend" who had allegedly been van der Sloot's accomplice in the dumping of Natalee's body. According to Daury, there was no way it could have happened that way because he was at school in Rotterdam on the day Natalee went missing.

When questioned by Dutch investigators about his startling confession, van der Sloot denied the things he had told van der Erm were true. He blamed the marijuana, claiming he only said what van der Erm had wanted to hear. Criticism erupted over the handling of the tapes, causing some to say they had been manipulated and edited to make it seem as if van der Sloot had confessed to a crime that did not happen. Others, however, were very critical of Peter R. de Vries, saying that his airing of the tapes made it impossible to use them as evidence against Joran van der Sloot. Had he thought of Natalee first instead of his own ratings and given the tapes to the authorities before broadcasting them, it's possible they could have aided the investigation instead of now further hindering it.

However, Joran van der Sloot was not yet done with adding new wrinkles to his story. Later that year, on November 28, van der Sloot told Fox News' Greta Van Susteren that he had sold Natalee Holloway into sexual slavery and had paid off the Kalpoe brothers for their assistance and silence. He alleged that Natalee had been taken to Venezuela and that his own father, the esteemed Aruban judge, Paulus van der Sloot had paid off a pair of Aruban cops.

van der Sloot told Van Susteren that two days before meeting Natalee Holloway, a man he had met in an Aruban casino had given Joran his number and told him to call if he ever was able to deliver a "blonde girl." According to van der Sloot, after leaving Carlos 'n Charlies with Natalee and the Kalpoe brothers, he called the man, speaking in Dutch so that she wouldn't understand. The man told van der Sloot to meet him in a parking lot just north of the Marriott in one hour.

When they arrived at the location, van der Sloot took Natalee to the beach where he claimed they began making out. Then, seemingly out of nowhere, another man showed up, handed van der Sloot a bag of cash and then grabbed Natalee by the arm. Because she was drunk and Joran had told her they were going on a boat, at first, she didn't struggle. It was only after the boat was speeding away from the beach that they heard her pleading voice asking what was going on.

After the Fox News interview aired, Joran van der Sloot, unsurprisingly, retracted the things he had told Van Susteren.

And yet, van der Sloot's lies don't end there. In February 2010, van der Sloot allegedly stated in yet another interview that he had dumped Natalee's body in a marsh. Then a month later, van der Sloot tried to extort two hundred fifty thousand dollars from Beth Twitty in exchange for revealing the true location of Natalee's body and the real circumstances around her death. According to documents from Interpol, a representative of Beth Twitty's family met with Joran van der Sloot in Aruba with ten thousand dollars in cash. An additional fifteen thousand dollars was wired to a bank account in the Netherlands with the rest to be paid if the information panned out. van der Sloot, who was living in Peru at the time, gave them a new version of his old song and dance—more false information. The house he claimed Natalee's body had been hidden in hadn't even been built at the time of her disappearance.

Unbeknownst to van der Sloot, the entire monetary transaction had been part of an FBI sting. Now they had enough to charge Joran van der Sloot with extortion and wire fraud. What happened next, however, would shock, but perhaps not surprise, many of those who had been involved in the case since the beginning.

Five years to the day after Natalee Holloway's disappearance, a pretty, young twenty-one-year-old student named Stephany Flores Ramirez was reported missing in Lima. Three days later, Stephany's body was discovered lying half-dressed on the floor of Joran van der Sloot's room at the Hotel Tac.

A receptionist had received a phone call for van der Sloot around eleven p.m. on June 1. When she forwarded the call and got no answer from his room phone, the receptionist noticed van der Sloot's account was two days past due. She went up to his room and knocked on the door. No one responded and the television was blaring so she used a master key to enter the room. To her horror, Stephany lay dead, dressed in only a black tee shirt and red panties, her neck broken, blood from her nose pooled on the floor.

After fleeing to Chile, some six hundred fifty miles away, Joran van der Sloot was arrested and confessed to her murder. He and Stephany had met the previous night, ironically enough, in a local casino. They returned to his hotel room. There, after she had allegedly used his laptop to find out about his involvement in the Natalee Holloway case, van der Sloot flew into a rage.

"We argued and she tried to escape. I grabbed her by the neck and I hit her," he confessed. "The girl intruded into my private life. She had no right."

In January of 2012, after entering his guilty plea in a Peruvian court of law, Joran van der Sloot was sentenced to twenty-eight years in prison, minus time served, and ordered to pay two hundred thousand dollars solace for civil reparations. Currently, he is scheduled to be released on June 10, 2038.

One can only be certain that it is a hollow and bitter victory for Beth Twitty to see van der Sloot locked away under such shockingly similar circumstances involving violence against young women. Only time will tell if the true whereabouts of Natalee Holloway will ever be revealed.

And even there, in a Peruvian jail, van der Sloot's stories about Natalee Holloway's disappearance continue to change. According to news sources, a Peruvian prison informant claims that van der Sloot told him that he had killed Natalee Holloway because she refused to have sex with him. After she slapped him, van der Sloot allegedly became angered and strangled her. van der Sloot then allegedly confessed to burying Natalee in a shallow sandy grave while she was barely conscious. Worried that she would soon be discovered, van der Sloot said he paid off a funeral home worker to hide Natalee Holloway's body in the coffin of an Aruban who was set to be interred in an above-ground tomb the following day.

Whether it is true or not, along with the allegations that Joran's father Paulus used his money and connections to cover up the crime, may never be known for certain. Though Paulus van der Sloot died from a heart attack in early 2010, still lingering is one remaining tidbit mentioned by Deepak Kalpoe that was never properly investigated.

According to Kalpoe, in the early morning hours after Natalee Holloway's disappearance, Paulus van der Sloot allegedly made two ATM transactions between three and four a.m. The authorities never asked why.

ALOHA MEANS GOODBYE

Aloha.

In the Hawaiian language it means hello and it also means goodbye. For David Potts, when tragedy struck on the Hawaiian Isles, it happened too fast for him to even let out a yell for help.

The drive up the West Maui coastline is breathtaking as you come up around the picturesque Nakalele Point. It's the northernmost tip of an island known for its stunning beauty and some of the best beaches in the world. Two and a half million visitors come just to Maui alone. Many make the circuitous journey along Highway 30, past sleepy Oluwalu and its General Store with perhaps the finest Spam Musubi in the state. Ask behind the counter and they will tell you the popular snack and lunch treat comprised of a slice of Spam grilled in a teriyaki sauce placed atop a block of rice and wrapped in seaweed is known around these parts as a "Hawaiian energy bar."

Continue up the coast, past Lahaina, the old whaling town turned into a tourist haven, past the sublime, sun-drenched golden shores of Kaanapali Beach. Soon, the congestion begins to fade as you pass upscale Napili and the resorts at Kapalua. Eventually, you will cross into the undeveloped edge of West Maui, up to Honolua Bay, home to crystalline water and coral reefs teeming with sea-life, making it a desired destination for snorkelers despite its rocky shoreline.

It is here, far away from the hotels, condo buildings and restaurants, where you can see the natural beauty of Maui in its pristine state.

Through the winding path of Highway 30, visitors make the trek just past mile marker 38 to see Nakalele Point. In particular, they park and descend a rocky, steep trail to come see the blowhole.

Formed by ancient eruptions of Maui Komohana, the West Maui Volcano, (the island's volcanic twin to the more famous Mt. Haleakela) Naklele Point is a lava shelf that juts out from the shoreline. When waves crash into the underside of Naklele Point, it forces water and air through a lava tube, causing fantastic geyser-like eruptions. Depending upon the size and strength of the tide, the sprays can reach up to one hundred feet into the air.

When the surf is pounding, as it was on the afternoon of July 9, 2011, the blowhole is truly a wonder to behold. It was then that San Anselemo, California contractor David Potts, forty-four, wearing only a pair of multi-colored floral printed board shorts and a gray hat, began to dance next to the blowhole, frolicking in the ocean spray.

One man, Rocco Piganelli from LaJolla California, snapped a photo of his daughter. In the background, he captured the last image of David Potts. Moments later, a violent wave crashed over the point, knocking Potts off his feet and into the blowhole. As water erupted from the hole, Potts' head bobbed to the surface for a fleeting second before the force of the outgoing tide sucked him down into the jagged, murky darkness.

Piganelli and several other shocked onlookers quickly scrambled over the rocks and rushed to the edge of the water to see if Potts would wash out with the tide.

But he was nowhere to be found.

It was then that the sister-in-law of Potts' longtime girlfriend let out a horrifying scream.

As it turned out, Pott's girlfriend, Tika Hick was not at the blowhole. She and David had traveled to Maui as their last hurrah before she was to undergo a double mastectomy in order to rid her body of the cancer that threatened her life. To make matters even worse, the diagnosis had come only weeks after the couple lost their house.

Three days later, the search, conducted by air and jet ski and complicated by rough waters and poor visibility, was finally called off.

Though cited in many Maui guidebooks, and a favorite sightseeing recommendation of hotel concierges, visiting the blowhole is always predicated with a warning to stay a safe distance from the ocean spray. Despite internet rumor that claims a warning sign in the parking lot says to stay at least twenty yards away, in fact, the only signage is a hand-lettered board that reads, "Blowhole Park And Walk At Your Own Risk."

Because the blowhole is on privately owned land, visitation to it is technically constituted as trespassing, though never enforced. The county of Maui claimed no responsibility for David Potts' death since neither they nor the Visitor's Bureau promotes the blowhole as an attraction.

That lack of liability, however, was not the case in the deaths of two female hikers who plunged three hundred feet from a Kauai trail in December 2006.

Thirty-five-year-old Elizabeth Brem, a vivacious, young attorney from Encinitas, California and doting mother of two young sons, had been planning the trip to Kauai with her cousin, Paula Gonzolez Ramirez, twenty-nine, of Columbia for the better part of a year. It would be the pair's first trip to the Garden Isle.

On December 19, the first day of their vacation, Elizabeth and Paula arrived at Wailua River State Park on the eastern side of the island. Here, visitors can take riverboat cruises, kayak along the Wailua River and explore the dense Kauai rainforest. In ancient times, this was the center of chiefly power on the island. According to Hawaiian historians, Wailua was King Kamehameha's most favorite of places to live. Among the many attractions in the park is the Wailua Complex, the site of several important ancient structures including the ruins of several heiau (places of worship). It is said that ghost warriors known as the *huakai po* stalk the river trails at night.

It was at the trailhead at Opaeka'a Falls that Elizabeth and Paula saw the split pathway. Though the trail on the left was well known as a route that led to a scenic pool below, there was a sign that read, "Danger Keep Out Hazardous Conditions."

The trail on the right had no sign.

Elizabeth and Paula took the right hand trail and ended up falling through a thick growth of foliage to their deaths.

The wet climate of Kauai is what creates such dense greenery, hence the nickname, "The Garden Isle." However, it is the thick foliage that grows up and out, in some cases twenty feet past the edges of cliffs, that can obscure the precipitous drop offs. It may look safe but since it won't hold the body weight of a normal human, one could unknowingly step from solid ground onto a fragile shelf made up solely of vegetation and plummet right through.

Elizabeth and Paula's bodies were found at the base of the cliff, thirty-five feet from the falls. In April, 2011, a Kauai judge ruled that the state was "100 percent at fault" in their deaths. In her forty-four-page decision, Judge Kathleen Watanabe ruled that the placement of the sign was worse than placing no sign at all.

The kicker is that only six months before the tragic and ultimately preventable deaths of Elizabeth Brem and Paula Ramirez, a sixteen-year-old boy fell from the same cliff. Joshua Lineras testified at the nine-day trial that he'd been hiking with his family when he also took the right hand trail. According to Lineras, there was a false floor and he fell one hundred fifty to two hundred feet without realizing there was a cliff. Though seriously injured, Lineras miraculously survived.

In a sad and tragically ironic note, at the beginning of 2006, Elizabeth Brem had been appointed to the board of the California Coastal Conservancy, an agency that helps raise funding to preserve coastal resources. In 2007, the Elizabeth Brem Memorial Fund was established at Yale Law School, her alma mater, in order to help female Hispanic students in need of financial aid.

There are indeed a number of treacherous hiking trails on Kauai, especially those along the gorgeous emerald cliffsides of the Na Pali Coast. Facilities are rugged. Trail beds are often narrow and crumbly and the island's abundant rainfall can make footing akin to walking on a slip-n-slide. Some eroded areas hug cliffs hundreds of feet above churning surf where a fall would turn a human body into hamburger against the jagged rocks below.

The breathtaking beauty of the Na Pali Coast is what draws many to Kauai. The garden paradise of the island's tropical settings has been used as the backdrops for movies like "Jurassic Park" and "Raiders of the Lost Ark." Rugged outdoorsman Daniel Marks, twenty-four, loved hiking, having conquered trails in New Zealand, Australia, Central America, India and in places like Yellowstone and the Grand Canyon. Often, he would venture off on extended camping trips, always returning home when promised. His trip to Kauai had been a last-minute jaunt the week before his sister's wedding spurred on by a cheap flight forwarded to his email from a friend. From San Francisco, he switched planes in Los Angeles and landed in Kauai on Wednesday November 9, 2005. He didn't even tell his family where he was going.

The trip was only scheduled to last a week. Instead, Daniel Marks never returned home.

After bunking at a hostel, the following day Daniel bummed a ride to the Kalalau Valley, a place where rainbows are often born from the constant whirls of mist and sunshine. At approximately four thirty in the afternoon, he had a short conversation with a Colorado couple also taking in the stunning northward sea views from a lookout on the Pihea trail where the jagged mountain terrain frames the valley. High above four thousand-foot drops on both sides, Daniel impressed his new acquaintances with his tenacious desire to get down the mountain before sunset. With a backpack slung over his shoulders and a walking stick in hand, he set off for the eastern ridge and was never seen again.

For ten days, nobody even realized Daniel was missing. All his mother knew of this most recent trip was that he was due to fly into Minneapolis on November 20 so he could visit her for Thanksgiving. After not finding him in the terminal on that date, she was given the news that Daniel was not on his flight. It was only after his sister Sue hacked into Daniel's email account that the family discovered where he had gone last.

Sue, along with Daniel's brother Ron Jr., arrived in Kauai on Thanksgiving Day, 2005. When they reported Daniel's disappearance to the local police, they were dismayed to see the case handled with what they viewed as complete indifference. To them, Daniel was treated as just another mainlander who had come looking for a wild adventure that was beyond his capacity and somehow vanished.

The Marks family took matters into their own hands. They hired professional search teams to comb the area for any sign of Daniel. At one point, a footprint thought to belong to Daniel, was found on one of the upper ridges, but the trail stopped there.

After papering the island with fliers featuring Dan's photo, they would eventually learn something ominous. Other men had gone missing near the same location.

On January 25, 2004, twenty-eight-year-old Bradford Turek parked his rental car at Ke'e Beach and went hiking along the Kalalu trail also never to be seen again.

Jesse Pinegar, twenty-three, had come to Kauai from Utah in January 2008. He hiked into the Kalalu Valley and set up a campsite. Though Jesse had remained in contact with his family back home, March 24 was the last time they heard from him before he, too, vanished.

In each case, Kauai police claim extensive aerial and ground searches were conducted. They say there is no reason to believe foul play was involved despite common knowledge of heavily armed gangs of squatters who illegally grow marijuana in the Valley and have been known to attack and injure those unsuspecting trespassers who have gotten too close. For now, the cases remain open and the men continue to be classified only as "missing."

One can only hope that someday clues will be found to end the nightmare of waiting and finally give these grieving families some type of closure.

In April 2010, search teams found the body of twenty-six-year-old Orem, Utah resident Ryan Soper nine days after he had had tumbled from a tree near Secret Falls in Wailua River Park. Soper, who weighed two hundred forty pounds, landed on his mother-in-law, breaking her ankle before his head and shoulders smashed hard against a rock. While the group he was with attended to his mother-in-law, Soper, disoriented and unknowingly suffering a concussion, wandered away. His body was discovered by Kauai resident John Bohling, laying face down at the base of a waterfall upstream from where he had first injured himself.

It took over a week to locate the body of forty-five-year-old Rancho Santa Margarita resident Nola Rebecca Thompson. The trip had been one she had been planning with her fiancée of several years. After they broke up, "Becky" as her friends called her, decided she would still go, even if it meant changing her seat on the plane and staying at a different hotel. The breakup was very difficult on Becky. According to friends, she turned heavily to religion in the ensuing weeks. Just five days before leaving, she left the following Facebook post: "I have forgiven everyone and now just want to be set free with God's grace and be at peace in my heart and mind."

On August 28, 2010, Becky arrived in Kauai three days before her birthday. She spoke to friends via telephone, including her former fiancée and his family who all wished her well.

Two days later, when Becky was supposed to leave, her rental car was nowhere to be found and all of her belongings remained in her hotel room.

After a multi-agency search including police and fire crews, along with a canine rescue team, Becky's silver Chrysler Sebring convertible was found on September 8 off of Kuamo'o Road in Wailua Homesteads in a remote area used for hiking. The next morning, at nine eighteen a.m, Becky's lifeless body was discovered face down in a stream two miles away. Due to extensive decomposition, Becky could only be identified through dental records.

No wounds were found on the body. Though an autopsy was performed, no cause of death was ever released.

Even though there was no evidence of foul play. Nola Rebecca Thompson's death remains curious, especially in light of the fact that a serial killer had been suspected in the slaying deaths of two women and an attack on a third on the island back in 2000. Of those murders, two of the victims were residents, one was visiting the island. Forty-three-year-old New York native Daryn Singer was an avid surfer who had come to Kauai looking to conquer its towering waves. In August of that year, she had arrived on the Garden Isle on the last stop of a hiking expedition before heading to Florida where she planned to help care for her ailing grandmother. A devotee of Krishna, Singer was an artist known to make stained glass and jewelry from sea shells.

Like thirty-eight-year-old Kauai resident Lisa Bissell, Daryn Singer was found sexually assaulted and stabbed to death. Severely beaten, Daryn was discovered partially-clothed, lying near foliage at her campsite near Pakala Beach, a popular, but remote surfing area. Because a small amount of cash was found among Daryn's belongings, robbery was not suspected as the motive in the attack.

Lisa Bissell's murder happened only a few miles away. A third victim, a fifty-two-year-old woman, was attacked at a secluded beach house in nearby Kekaha. Though being stabbed in the abdomen and suffering a broken arm, she fought off her attacker and managed to survive. A suspect has never been apprehended.

Curious though is that ten years later, another suspicious and similar murder occurred on Kauai. Fifty-seven-year-old Amber Jackson's body was found in a wooded area in Kealia. The fact that Amber had been assaulted much like the victims in the rash of attacks a decade earlier has led some to wonder if the Kauai serial rapist and killer was on the prowl once again.

Of course, it is not only Kauai that has seen its share of recent tourist killings. Twenty-five-year-old aspiring actress Bryanna Antone was visiting Oahu from Rio Rancho, New Mexico with her brother and her mother, who was in Hawaii attending an American Dental Association convention in Waikiki. While listening to a band on the night of October 1, 2009, Bryanna and her brother met a thirty-one-year-old man named Aaron Susa. Appearing to hit it off, the three went to a nearby convenience store where they purchased alcohol before going back to Bryanna's room at the Waikiki West Hotel. After consuming a number of drinks, Bryanna and Susa began making out on the bed.

Bryanna's brother left the room around one a.m. to get food. When he returned, his sister, along with her new acquaintance, were both gone. An hour later, Bryanna, still drunk, called to tell her brother that she was down on the beach.

Shortly after six a.m. the following morning, Bryanna's naked body washed up on Waikiki beach. DNA found on her body quickly led them to Susa, who claimed the pair had sex on the beach and then in the ocean. The coroner's report listed the cause of death as drowning. Her body was also found with a fractured larynx and bruises on her neck and chest. Witnesses reported seeing a man and woman arguing and then struggling on the beach.

The night they met, Susa told Bryanna that some twelve hours beforehand, he had been released from prison after spending four months in jail for harassing a police officer. Whether he had also divulged that he had spent at least a year of his life behind bars for arrests on drug-related charges and unauthorized entry into a motor vehicle or that he had mostly lived on the streets is unknown.

Over two years later, on November 7, 2011, a jury found Aaron Michael Susa guilty of second-degree murder, a crime that carries a mandatory life sentence with the chance of parole.

It should be said that not all vacation murders are perpetrated by locals. On September 1, 2011 police responded to calls about a domestic dispute at Maui's Nakalele Point off Kahekili Highway, a narrow, winding road that begins where Highway 30 ends. There they discovered thirty-eight-year-old Gerald Galaway. When police attempted to question the six foot three-inch tall, two hundred pound Galaway, he bolted and jumped from a one hundred-foot high cliff into the ocean. Galaway was found the next morning and airlifted to a hospital with non-life-threatening injuries.

The body of Galaway's companion, thirty-five-year-old Santa Cruz attorney, Celestial Cassman was later discovered under a tree at the bottom of a cliff. Her shirt was ripped and there was evidence of sexual assault.

Cassman and Galaway had arrived on Maui a day earlier and were staying in Kaanapali Beach. While driving up the coast, the couple got into a fierce argument and the car swerved and stopped on the side of the road. When a local woman pulled up to see if she could offer some assistance, Cassman threw the rental car keys to her and yelled for help. It was then that Galaway became extremely violent. After getting Cassman into a headlock, he slammed her head against the road. Horrified, the local woman drove down the road to find a phone where she called the police who showed up too late to save Cassman's life.

The pair had been dating for several years.

Though violence has taken the life of a small handful of Hawaiian visitors, by far the most dangerous thing on the islands is the water. That postcard-pretty effervescent blue ocean is catnip for the soul, an irresistible draw for millions that can occasionally spell danger for unsuspecting surfers, snorkelers, divers or kayakers.

One of the most lasting perceived threats to humans off the shores of Hawaii are sharks. Between the years 1828 to 2005, there have been one hundred nineteen documented shark attacks in the waters off Hawaii. Only twenty-one were fatal. Out of the some 7.5 million visitors that come to the Aloha State each year, that represents a nearly inconsequential fraction.

Inconsequential, as long as it's not you, of course. And as recorded statistics show, nearly all fatal shark attack victims in Hawaii have been Hawaiians. Perhaps the finned predators haven't developed a taste for Coppertone and Crocs.

But just because shark attacks are as rare as fatal lightning strikes doesn't mean it doesn't happen.

In March of 1999, thirty-nine-year-old Mark Monazzami, an Iranian-born computer engineer from Sunnyvale, California, arrived in Maui for a belated honeymoon with his bride, twenty-nine-year-old Nahid Davoobadabi. Like many West Maui visitors, they rented a kayak to explore the shoreline. However, it was a trip that would end in disaster.

The seas were calm. Monazzami and Davoobadabi stayed close to the beach, but unexpectedly strong winds kicked up, blowing the pair far from shore. Before they knew it, Monazzami and his wife were in over their heads, literally, as the blowing gusts capsized their kayak several times while they struggled to get back to land. By nightfall, the current had taken the heavily fatigued pair deep into the channel between Maui and neighboring Molokai as they clung to the overturned kayak trying to stay out of the chilly wind.

When danger struck, it came quickly. "Shark!" shouted Davoobadabi just before being pulled under. In moments, the ocean was red. Her arm was missing, having been bitten off. Monazzami tried to pull her aboard the kayak. Unable to control the bleeding, he could only cradle her as she died. Buffeted by strong winds in the rough seas, he was unable to hold onto her. Sometime during the night, her body slipped into the water and vanished.

Drifting on the kayak overnight, Monozzami made it to the rocky shore of Kaho'olawe, an uninhabited island owned by the government and used for munitions testing. After wandering for two days, Monozzami came across an old military bunker. Inside, by some small miracle, was a working telephone.

After being airlifted back to Maui, he recounted his tale to authorities who listed the incident as an unconfirmed shark attack. Davoobadabi's body was never recovered and some who doubt Monozzami's tale have speculated that he may have instead murdered his wife.

Much luckier was Julie Glance, a thirty-four-year-old credit union CEO who had come from San Diego to Maui with her family in October of

2002. Swimming one hundred fifty yards from shore along the Kaanapali coastline just off the beach at the Embassy Suites where she was staying, Julie felt something bump into her and cut into her shoulder.

A second bite came just seconds later before the shark was gone, taking some bone from Julie's shoulder with it. More life-threatening though were the deep cuts in her right hand and wrist and the severed artery and tendons. Before it left, Julie got a good look at the shark. It was six feet long, grey in color with a white tipped tail.

Bleeding profusely, Julie swam back to shore. Two hours of surgery saved her life.

As much as shark attacks grab the headlines and terrify the terrify-able, it is not *Jaws* that Hawaiian ocean swimmers should fear as much as the water itself. This often-underestimated power of the ocean and currents in and around Hawaii along with the propensity for tourists to engage in "high risk" activities that they may have only done a few times before or never, can easily turn into a lethal combination.

On average, sixty people drown each year in Hawaii. Half of those are tourists.

By far, drowning is the leading cause of unintentional death by injury for those under the age of fourteen.

Hawaii State Department of Health statistics show that roughly half of all island tourist drownings happen in Oahu, home of popular Waikiki Beach and Pearl Harbor. In March of 2011, KHON Channel 2, reported that an unidentified

Canadian woman in her fifties was wading in the ocean near tranquil Ke Iki Beach when a rogue wave swept her and two family members into the ocean. Though the two family members were rescued by bystanders, the woman was pulled out to sea by the strong undertow. Her lifeless body was discovered later by lifeguards. The ocean conditions at the time were considered to be hazardous.

It should be noted that David Potts was also not in the ocean when the massive wave that crashed over the rocks knocked him down into the Nakalele Point Blowhole.

Extremely strong currents and rough seas are not uncommon and even for strong swimmers, can be very dangerous. Five people drowned off of Kauai in December of 2010 alone. Two of those deaths occurred in one day. Corey Dunn, twenty, of North Carolina drowned while snorkeling in a bay near Po'ipū Beach. Forty-one-year old Jason Fleiss, brother of former Hollywood madam Heidi Fleiss, drowned at Kauapea Beach near Kīlauea.

If one is to believe a handmade sign hanging at the remotely located Hanakapiai Beach on Kauai's Na' Pali Coast, dozens of visitors have lost their lives along this picturesque stretch of sand due to strong rip currents, high surf and hazardous shore breaks. As of December of 2008, a scratched-in tally below the words: "Hanakapiai Beach Warning! Do Not Go Near The Water. Unseen Currents Have Killed" exceeds eighty-three slashes.

Even away from the ocean itself, drowning still poses many dangers.

Kauai's Kipu Falls is often described by guidebooks and websites as a hidden gem off the beaten path, a swimming hole with the alluring beauty of a waterfall and natural pool. What few ever mention is the site's deadly reputation.

Between 2006 and 2011, five people drowned at Kipu Falls.

Swimmers routinely make the twenty-foot-high jump from the top of the falls into the crystal waters of the pool. The unlucky few who died were pulled under as they attempted to swim to shore. On June 26, 2011, thirty-five-year-old Santhosh Heddese from Irvine, California made the leap at five minutes past two p.m. He struggled, trying to escape the falls before going underwater and never resurfacing.

Divers recovered his body from the bottom of the pool an hour later. Some suspect there is a strong whirlpool current below the falls that acts as a suction. Others, especially locals, believe that an angry *mo'o*, or Hawaiian water spirit lizard, lurks in the deep waters below Kipu Falls.

Kipu Falls is on private property. In 2011, due to public outcry and threat of lawsuits, the owners of the land erected a fence to keep trespassers out... and safe.

Though very few warnings were ever issued about the dangers of Kipu Falls, the same cannot be said about other Hawaiian tourist tragedies that possibly could have been avoided.

Back in April of 2003, thirty-nine-year old Louisville, Kentucky schoolteacher Kevin Brown was on a spring break vacation with his family and parents. On a lightly rainy day, they drove the twisty roads of the Hana Highway, ending up at East Maui's Haleakela National Park. There they planned to see the very popular O'heo Gulch, known also as the Seven Sacred Pools, a cascading series of stunning waterfalls and freshwater pools that flow into the ocean. In the previous twenty-four hours, an inch of rain had fallen at O'heo. The National Weather Service had posted a flash-flood warning at four twenty-five p.m.

At four thirty, Brown, his wife, son and eight-year-old daughter Elizabeth were hiking alongside the Pipiwai Trail when they decided to cross the stream. Elizabeth lost her footing and slipped. As Brown tried to help her up, the family of four heard a deafening roar.

A six foot tall wall of water unleashed from swelling upstream pools washed down the O'heo Gulch. Caught in its destructive path were Brown and Elizabeth who were both swept over the one hundred eighty-four-foot tall Makahiku Falls to their deaths.

There was no time to say, "aloha," only to scream.

There is little doubt Hawaii is one of the most beautiful and relaxing places on earth to take a vacation. There is so much to do. The people, for the most part, are extremely friendly and the sun, air and water will be things you will think about every day for the rest of your life. It would be grossly unfair to characterize Hawaii as unsafe based solely upon the tragic stories of the handful of tourists who have died there. However, like anywhere else you travel, there are risks you undertake with certain activities—risks that will hopefully not prevent you from returning home with anything other than pleasant memories and a deep tan.

*****

TOP 10 "DARE TO BE AWARE" TRAVEL TIPS I LEARNED WRITING FATAL SUNSET

Tip 1: Never assume you have the same rights, protections and access to emergency services in other countries as you do in your own.

Tip 2: Take the time to check out any attractions your children may use before you leave them unsupervised.

Tip 3: Always let someone know where you're going and how long you'll be gone. If you're on a trip, make sure someone in your party knows when you'll be back and check in with them if those plans change.

Tip 4: Don't assume that video cameras are there to protect you - They are only there to protect the interests of the property owners who may have a different agenda when it comes to revealing what those cameras have seen.

Tip 5: Just because there isn't a warning sign, doesn't mean there isn't danger - Use your common sense and/or double check your plans with someone who knows the lay of the land.

Tip 6: Do your research - Any reputable company offering trips, excursions, tours will have a digital footprint on the Internet. Use Google to search for reviews before you use them.

Tip 7: Be suspicious of anyone who takes too much interest in you or your family - If someone you really don't know invites you to join them in an excursion somewhere, don't be afraid to turn them down. There are worse things than offending someone who you will probably never see again.

Tip 8: If going out of the country, check for government issued travel advisories for your destination. If the state department says someplace is unsafe, take heed.

Tip 9: Being on vacation doesn't turn you into Superman - Don't try doing anything that may be more physically involved than something you would do at home.

Tip 10: Always listen and be kind to your flight attendant - He or she has much more experience than you in dealing with onboard emergencies and situations. Their help could save your life!

*****

ACKNOWLEDGEMENTS

Special thanks goes out to: Maureen Webster over at *MexicoVacationAwareness.com* for her help with my research and for being wonderfully brave in allowing me to interview her about such a difficult topic.

The one and only P.W. Fenton.

Christie over at *EbookEditingPro.com* for the critical eye.

To my wonderful family with whom I always have the best vacations ever.

And of course, as always, a big, big thanks to those of you who continue to buy, recommend and support my books!

BOOKS BY MARK YOSHIMOTO NEMCOFF

NON-FICTION:
- The Killing of Osama Bin Laden: How the Mission to Hunt Down a Terrorist Mastermind was Accomplished
- Where's My F*cking Latte? (And Other Stories About Being an Assistant in Hollywood)
- Go Forth and Kick Some Ass (Be the Hero of Your Own Life Story)
- Pacific Coast Hellway Presents - Pissed Off: Is Better Than Being Pissed On
- Admit You Hate Yourself

FICTION:
- Diary of a Madman
- The Doomsday Club
- The Art of Surfacing
- Number One with a Bullet
- Shadow Falls: Badlands
- Shadow Falls: Angel of Death
- Killing My Boss
- Transistor Rodeo
- INFINITY

ABOUT THE AUTHOR

Mark Yoshimoto Nemcoff is a bestselling and award-winning author who has been known to occasionally moonlight as a voice-over artist and independent journalist. He is a former Sirius Satellite Radio drive time show and T.V. host that has been featured by Playboy Magazine and Access Hollywood. He is the writer behind Kindle bestsellers "The Death of Osama Bin Laden" and "Where's My F***ing Latte?", an insiders look at the world of Hollywood celebrity assistants that was not only featured on Access Hollywood, but has spent over four years straight at the top of Amazon's top-selling chart in the categories of "Television" and "Movies."

Mark currently resides in Los Angeles.

He can be reached at: MYN@WordSushi.com
Twitter.com/MYN
Facebook.com/MYNBooks

If you enjoyed this book, please tell your friends.
                                                                -MYN

Made in the USA
Lexington, KY
28 June 2012